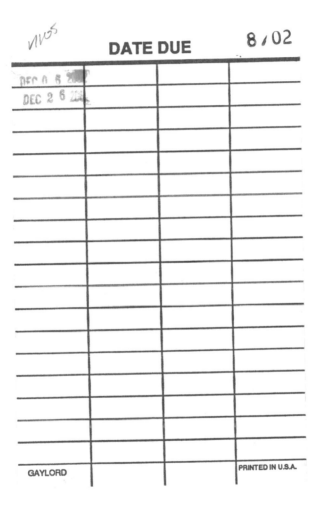

DATE DUE

8/02

DEC 0 6 20			
DEC 2 6 20			
GAYLORD			PRINTED IN U.S.A.

If It Bleeds, It Leads

If It Bleeds, It Leads

An Anatomy of Television News

Matthew R. Kerbel

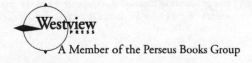

Westview
PRESS

A Member of the Perseus Books Group

Copyright © 2000 by Westview Press, A Member of the Perseus Books Group

Published in 2000 in the United States of America by Westview Press, 5500 Central Avenue, Boulder, Colorado 80301-2877, and in the United Kingdom by Westview Press, 12 Hid's Copse Road, Cumnor Hill, Oxford OX2 9JJ

Find us on the World Wide Web at www.westviewpress.com

Library of Congress Cataloging-in-Publication Data
Kerbel, Matthew Robert, 1958-
  If it bleeds, it leads : an anatomy of television news / Matthew Robert Kerbel.
    p.   cm.
  Includes bibliographical references and index.
  ISBN 0-8133-6836-7
  1. Television broadcasting of news.   I. Title.
PN4784.T4 K47   2000
070.1'95—dc21   99-052384

The paper used in this publication meets the requirements of the American National Standard for Permanence of Paper for Printed Library Materials Z39.48-1984.

10   9   8   7   6   5   4   3   2

For Adrienne and Gabrielle

Rundown

Disclaimer

WARNING: Everything you are about to read is true.

The following chapters contain graphic content that may not be suitable for all readers. Some of the material is of a violent or sexual nature. You may encounter descriptions of bizarre or antisocial acts, committed out of desperation by despondent individuals. There will be accounts of frightening conditions and descriptions of portentous situations, which may make you feel threatened, fearful, endangered, jeopardized, or at risk. Some of the imagery described to you will be disturbing.

That's because you will be watching the news.

You are about to embark on a real-time journey through two-and-a-half hours of talk and news programming, taken from actual shows that were broadcast in syndication, on local television stations, and on the major networks. My purpose is to go behind the pictures and words to see what local and network news stories are really about. Television news is as familiar as the paint on the wall—but can it be we've also been taking in hidden messages we never knew were there? We'll find out.

We rely on television. Television helps us make sense of the world. It helps us figure out what's important. It helps us get close to people we would otherwise never meet. It shows us events that we would otherwise never experience. What would happen to our perception of life around us if television has been missing most of what really matters all these years? Is it possible that the closer we look at television news, the more it disappears? It's an anatomy of television news, up close and personal, as you've never seen it before. And it starts—now.

Remember: Everything you are about to read is true.

Everything appearing in italics was originally broadcast on television. At times you may find yourself shaking your head in disbelief at something you read. You may find yourself thinking, "This is too unbelievable to be real."

So, it bears repeating: Everything in italics was originally broadcast on a television talk, local news, or network news program.

What you are about to read is a composite of real material actually broadcast nationally or in select cities around the country. We'll begin with a selection from popular talk shows—because, as we'll soon see, Sally, Jerry, Ricki, Jenny, and Montel have a lot in common with Dan, Peter, Tom, and your favorite local news anchors. The guests we'll meet are real, and their situations will be represented exactly as they appeared on television.

Next, we'll see a composite version of your early evening newscast, featuring real stories from four of the largest U.S. media markets: Los Angeles, Philadelphia, Phoenix, and Detroit. All the stories you'll see were broadcast during the same week in at least one of these cities.

Finally, we'll turn to a composite version of the national news, featuring selections from ABC "World News Tonight," NBC "Nightly News," and "The CBS Evening News with Dan Rather." Except for stories about major past events, like the last presidential election and President Bill Clinton's impeachment, all the stories you will see aired during the same week on one of these three programs.

Because this is a composite, we'll have more anchors than we're used to seeing on one news set. In addition to Sally, Jerry, Ricki, Jenny, Montel, Dan, Peter, and Tom, we'll meet a team of local anchors from our four local markets. At times, Lisa and Harold from L.A. will toss a story to Marc or Robin or Carol from Phoenix, or to Larry or Ken from Philadelphia or Guy or Diana from Detroit. We'll have a host of weathercasters, sports reporters, and correspondents from all four cities as well. Think of it as an all-star team of local news personalities.

Because this book is not laid out in a traditional chapter format, the sections are delineated by air-time headings to emulate the way television broadcasting is structured. We'll begin our programming at 4:00 PM. with an hour of syndicated talk, followed by an hour of local news "Live at Five" and a half-hour of national news at 6:00 PM. This, too, is a composite. In your city, such syndicated talk shows as Montel Williams and Ricki Lake probably appear at different times, either earlier in the day or more likely throughout the afternoon on several different channels. You probably have an hour of news at 5:00 PM, but it may continue until 6:30 or start as early as 4:00. Your network news may be on earlier if you live in the Midwest or later if you live in the East. But the general flow of news and information that I describe mirrors what you'll find in most cities. And, remember—the stories depicted are real, and the names have not been changed.

You may have questions about my qualifications to lead you on this journey into the hidden side of television news. I am a former newswriter and a longtime observer of television. Let's say that I'm someone who has seen news operations from the inside and observed them from a distance. I've never been a television personality, but I have held jobs in broadcasting. If you wish to know more, you can read about me in the section titled "About the Author" in the back of the book. Likewise, if you're interested in knowing more about how this book was assembled, you can find what you need to know in the section in the back titled "Closing Comments."

Finally, please be advised that the publisher and I remind you to exercise discretion in the use of this book. Some of what you read may disturb you and may not be suitable for young children. This volume does not come equipped with a V-chip. Please use good judgment.

Hour One: Syndicated Talk

(The Actual Program You See Will Vary Depending on Where You Live)

4:00:00 PM: STATION IDENTIFICATION

You're watching Channel Seven, WXYZ Detroit, where Seven stands for news.

The "News Fifteen" investigators get results—KNXV Phoenix.

All new "Air Seven"—only on ABC/7, KABC-TV Los Angeles.

This is NBC/10, Philadelphia—your station for the new millennium.

4:00:05 PM: OPENING MONTAGE (ROLL TAPE)

The Jerry Springer Show may contain adult themes, strong language, or violence. Parents are cautioned that this program may not be appropriate for children. (**Audience:** Jer-ry!...Jer-ry!...Jer-ry!...Jer-ry!... Jer-ry!...Jer-ry!...Jer-ry!...Jer-ry!)

Jerry: *Thank you. Oh, gosh, bring tears to my eyes. Hey, welcome to the show!*

Face to face with the new woman...Babies caught in the middle...It's time for the test—I have to know...Who's your daddy? Today on Sally. (**Video:** Audience members standing and shouting; Sally waving her arms up and down.)

Bitter enemies face off...Who wrecked the friendship? Montel will find out. Betrayed by a best friend. Don't go away—that's coming up right now, on Montel. (**Video:** Audience applauds, kids laugh, adults laugh, Montel laughs, everybody laughs, someone cries, lots of people hug.)

4:00:35 PM: MEET THE HOSTS

Judging from all the laughing and hugging, we should have a good time. But before we meet the guests, let's take 5 minutes and say hello to some of the hosts who will guide us through the next two-and-a-half hours of television talk and information. What motivates these hosts to be at television's cutting edge as they relate the "Great Issues of Our Day"? After all, their views inevitably influence our views. So, it's worth taking a moment to consider the backgrounds of Jerry and Montel and Jenny and Ricki and Sally.

What's that? You say you're already familiar with them? Well, what about their second-act counterparts, Dan and Peter and Tom?

That's right, the serious news guys. They belong here, too.

You're wondering what they have to do with wrecked friendships, cheating spouses, and testosterone-primed audiences? Actually, a lot more than you may realize. Let's see how much you know about the people who have access to your living room any time you want to let them in.

Try a little matching game. First, connect the three biographies below to the correct news host:

BIOGRAPHY	HOST
1. This television personality was raised in Canada, did not complete college, and was recognized for the two-part special report, "AIDS in America, 1996."	a. Peter Jennings
2. An Annapolis graduate, this big-time host holds an engineering degree with a minor in international security affairs.	b. Dan Rather
3. A former big-city news anchor with a law degree from Northwestern University, this former staffer for Senator Robert F. Kennedy is consistently first or second in the ratings for his category.	c. Tom Brokaw

2

You're probably thinking number one is easy. Peter Jennings is Canadian, doesn't have a formal education, and always seems to be getting honored for something he's done. Dan Rather seems like the Annapolis type, and he appears to have a concern for international security affairs, so he must be the choice for number two. That would make Tom Brokaw the Northwestern law-school graduate and the former political hand. And that makes a lot of sense—he's from the Midwest and has an abiding interest in politics.

It all fits pretty well. Except these were trick questions. The Canadian host with the report on AIDS is Jenny Jones, not Peter Jennings. The Annapolis graduate isn't Dan Rather—he went to Sam Houston State University. It's really Montel Williams. And the lawyer with the Big Ten credentials who worked for Bobby Kennedy is Jerry Springer. Honest.

You see, talk show hosts and television anchors have a lot in common—probably a lot more than the anchors would like to admit. Maybe Ricki Lake didn't jet to Tibet to interview the Dalai Lama like Tom Brokaw did, and maybe she would have suggested a makeover if she had. But the talkers and anchors are cut from similar cloth.

They've all written books, and their books usually become best-sellers. Sally and Jerry once worked in local television news, just like Dan and Tom. Just about everybody's won an Emmy for something.

Unfortunately, most people don't recognize these connections. The talkers have a bad reputation, which for many people keeps them in lower regard than the news anchors. But, when you read their biographies, it's difficult to understand why. If anything, the talkers are the compassionate alter egos to the hard-hitting journalists. While Dan is off exhibiting his "tough, active style" by reporting from the middle of Hurricane Opal, the talkers are demonstrating their sensitivity to some of the same social issues covered in the news—the "Great Issues of Our Day."

Don't take my word for it. Ask them—or look at what they say about themselves in their biographies. Jenny's purpose in television life is to "entertain, enlighten, and often educate." Ricki heals social wounds, turning passive television viewing into "an hour of lively community interaction." Montel applies his "passionate and proactive" demeanor to "breaking news," sort of a healing version of Peter Jennings. Even controversial Jerry is misunderstood by people who are blind to his sensitive side—the side that "holds the hands of AIDS-stricken children, goes underground with New York's 'Mole People' who live in subway tunnels, and is the concerned humanitarian helping to raise millions of dollars for charity."

Sally is a "friend, confidante and adviser" who wonders aloud, through her Web site, "what makes [me] so empathetic?" Her answer: "I am the mother of grown children." I ask you—how can anyone argue with that? But, it must be more than her mom instincts that make Sally special, because she has assumed a burden few could carry. In her own words: "If I am in a strange city standing on a street corner, I'm the one people ask for directions. If I'm in a restaurant ladies room, the woman next to me automatically tells me the story of her life!" It's hard to imagine that happening to Dan Rather, and not because he doesn't frequent ladies rooms.

So, I'm visualizing Sally trying to plan for her next show while being bombarded by map-laden strangers who need the best route to the airport. She's summoning the sensitivity she needs to approach her guests and audience with the sort of respect she says we should expect from her. I'm imagining Jerry, fresh from a poignant visit with the "Mole People," ready to raise the consciousness of his studio audience. And, try as I might, I can't shake the image of Ricki offering a makeover to the Dalai Lama.

We are in good hands with these folks, provided that we never lose sight of their concerned humanitarian side. In saying that, I don't mean to slight Dan and Peter and Tom. They do good work, but it's not always uplifting. Sure, they've interviewed George Bush and Jesse Jackson—but so has Jerry Springer. Of course, the hard newsies help us make sense of our world, but not in the life-affirming way of Sally or Ricki.

Their guests should consider themselves lucky to be in the presence of giants.

4:05:00 PM: MEET THE GUESTS

Are the guests aware of their great luck in having such notable hosts? Unfortunately, I don't think so. Perhaps they're just too busy with their own problems.

Let's try to sort it out. Heaven is cheating on her boyfriend Billy by sleeping with Billy's friend Gary and Gary's girlfriend Lacy. Chautney, a transsexual prostitute, is cheating on Leasha, a female impersonator, by sleeping with Leasha's brother Jason. Mikki is an escort who cheats on her boyfriend by sleeping with her customers. Sandy has a crush on Rodney, and to prove it she's ready to shovel earthworms out of a box of dirt. Jeff wants to proclaim his infatuation with Erinn by drinking a mixture of tomato juice, hot sauce, pickle juice, and tuna. Twenty-year-old Toby wants to prove he's the father of ex-girlfriend Nikki's daughter Lacy, since he's already gone to the trouble of kidnapping Lacy from her Alabama home. For her part, Lacy may want to make sure you know that she's not the same person as the Lacy who is having an affair with Heaven.

And that's just Friday. Things get more complicated when you back up to Monday. Then, you find Willie, a bisexual, is cheating on his girlfriend by sleeping with a drag queen who is also named Willie, while bisexual Torrence is cheating on his transvestite girlfriend Seven (that's her name, not the channel designation) and Seven's boyfriend Jerry. Aries dumped his bisexual friend Jennifer after a threesome with Jennifer and Toya, but he's still with Toya. Erica dropped her boyfriend Mickey for her friend Sonya. Meanwhile, Eric is still in jail while his girlfriend Vera has moved on. Rosie Rockets and Chesty Love ponder their size M breasts, raising one of the most pressing social issues of our day: "Big-Breasted Women: Blessed or Cursed?" At the other end of the scale, Conrad talks about fooling women into believing she is a man, even though she is really a woman (named Connie). Salina challenges Kim while Dave challenges Rachel—they "Got to Know the Deal, 'Cuz I Don't Think That Body Part's Real."

On Tuesday, Sylvia is cheating on her husband Kenny by sleeping with Danny and Reggie, while Jeremy is cheating on his girlfriend Amy with Amy's cousin Shawna and DawnMarie is cheating on her boyfriend David with Eric—and Tammi. Sam may have been cheating on his twenty-two-year-old wife Erica, if the lie-detector test he took is correct. Will Erica resort to the same tactics as Caroline, who hired an undercover cop to kill her husband?

Wednesday brings us Charles, who sneaks out on his girlfriend Kim to be with his transsexual friend Moma. Ilana is cheating on her African-American boyfriend Brian with a Klan member. Jake is cheating on his gay boyfriend Jeff with his overweight buddy Tiny. Wild teens Courtney, Greg, and Keith run away, get arrested, steal for drugs, have sex, drink, carry weapons, and smoke pot.

On Thursday, Passion, Sommer, Collette, Ashley, Gummi, and Godiva feel compelled to announce to their friends and family members, "I Got Huge Breasts!" apparently because their friends and relatives are nearsighted. Yeko and Chara iron out who stole whose boyfriend. Engineering student Ruth gets a surprise makeover.

Then there's Big Daddy, who is cheating on his transsexual, phone-sex-operator girlfriend Christina, and twenty-nine-year-old Jim, who is cheating on his nineteen-year-old girlfriend Regina with thirty-eight-year-old Rhoda. Barry is cheating on his wife Dianne with his ex-wife Susan and his ex-girlfriend Melonie.

Bill is cheating on his wife Hillary by having an affair with Monica at work, although they are not sleeping together. Monica confides in her best friend Linda, who secretly records their phone conversations and hands them over to Kenneth, who doesn't think much of Bill and tries to get him fired. Bill admits to having been unfaithful hundreds of times with other women, including Gennifer and maybe Paula (who claims to have psychic powers), but he contends he always told the truth about what he did. Will Bill submit to a lie-detector test to settle, once and for all, "The Truth About My Outrageous Secret Lovers"?

Sorry, that one's not on "Montel." Let's wait two hours for Dan and Peter and Tom to give us their version of the "Great Issues of Our Day."

4:10:00 PM: SUPPLY MEDICAL TREATMENT FOR THE GUESTS

Now, if Dan and Peter and Tom would only let the people in their stories battle it out on stage, we might be spared having to listen to the same ugly details of their lives over and over for months at a time, not to mention the agony of having to listen to all those lawyers. The talkers figured out the secret before the newsies did: Don't change the story, change the characters. Resolve the problem and move on to the same problem with other people. Everyone's talking about the same things anyway, so it's not like the talk shows cover different ground than the news shows. The only difference is they move on more quickly to the next round. That, and they're more likely to feature people named Gummi.

Of course, there is a down side to the quick resolution of disputes. The talkers need to make sure they have enough units of their guests' blood types in reserve. This is something Dan and Peter and Tom don't have to worry about, providing Dan stays in his chair when he interviews George Bush.

It's a serious consideration. If those bouncers offstage don't respond quickly enough, guests could end up in an ambulance or, worse, on another talk show proclaiming, "I Got A Concussion on *Springer*!"

An incident can happen at any time, and probably will. Let's watch:

Jerry: *Meet Vixen. She says that she's come a long way to find out what her boyfriend has to tell her. She says it's time to be a real man and confess his secret.* (**Audience:** Wild applause.) *Vixen, uh, tell us about you. How long have you been with your boyfriend?*

Vixen: *Uh, me and Solo, we've been together for six months on and off. We get along, we go out, we have fun, it's like he's my best friend. I care about him a lot.*

Jerry (trying to understand): *So, you care about him?*

Vixen: *Yes, I do, a lot.* (**Audience:** Groans of empathy.)

Jerry: *And you think he's here because he wants to tell you something, and you're thinking, oh, this is going to be good.*

Vixen: *Yes, I'm really thinking…*(**Audience:** Shouts of apprehension; Vixen shakes her head.)

Jerry: *Well, every once in a while it's good news. I remember about eight years ago there was one story where there was good news, so we're due.* (**Audience:** Laughter; Vixen smiles.) *Well, let's meet your boyfriend. Here he is—Solo.* (Solo enters, embraces and kisses Vixen. Bouncers take their stations.)

Jerry: *Solo, welcome to the show.*

Solo: *How you doing, Jerry?*

Jerry: *Nice to meet you. Solo, interesting name. You alone a lot?* (**Audience:** laughter)

Solo: *Some of the time.*

Jerry: *Okay. What's the relationship doing?*

Solo: *Me and Vixen have been together for about six months on and off. We have a good relationship, like best friends. You know, we click.*

Jerry: *Is it romantic at all?*

Vixen: *Always.*

Solo: *Yeah.* (**Audience:** Groans.) *It's a connection, you know what I'm saying? Like we've known each other before, you know?*

Jerry: *Well great. Well, she's a little concerned that you say, hey, let's go on the "Jerry Springer Show," you've got something to tell her.* (**Audience:** Wild applause and shouting. Emergency medical technicians take note.) *What do you want to tell her?*

Solo (to Vixen): *Vixen, you know, I care about you, you know. You're a major part of my life, you know. We get along. You're there for me, and I didn't mean to hurt you, but, um, I slept with your sister.*

Vixen: *What? You what?* (**Audience:** Frenzied shouting. Vixen jumps up and begins punching Solo.)

The elapsed time of this exchange was 2 minutes and 20 seconds.

4:12:20 PM: BEGIN FIRST PROTRACTED SHOVING, PUNCHING, AND DELETED DIALOGUE SEGMENT BETWEEN BEST FRIENDS WHO CARE ABOUT EACH OTHER A LOT

4:13:15 PM: ADD FUEL TO FIRE; CUE SECOND BOUNCER

Jerry (to Vixen): *Actually, you've got something to ask your sister, too. Why she would, you know.*

Vixen: *You're damn right I do.*

Jerry: *Here she is, Kimberly.*

4:13:27 PM: BEGIN 2-MINUTE 45-SECOND SIBLING SHOVING, PUNCHING, AND DELETED DIALOGUE SEGMENT

4:16:12 PM: ADD MORE FUEL TO FIRE; ALERT HOSPITAL TO PREPARE FOR INJURIES

Jerry (to Solo): *There's something else you need to tell Vixen.*

Solo (to Vixen): *Yeah. I was born a woman.* (Solo and Vixen chase each other into the audience; bouncers follow; some audience members punch Solo while others, on their feet, chant: "Jer-ry!...Jer-ry!...Jer-ry!")

The elapsed time of this exchange was 1 minute and 50 seconds.

Jerry: *Okay, let's get back to the show.*

4:18:02 PM: EVERYONE REALIZES THIS IS THE SHOW

Jerry (to Solo): *You just told Vixen that you, in fact, were really a woman. But, Kimberly, you knew. Why wouldn't you tell your sister?* (**Audience:** Screaming and shouting; bouncers try for 40 seconds to separate Vixen and Kimberly; time for a commercial message.)

4:23:30 PM: PREPARE TO PAY BOUNCERS OVERTIME

Jerry: *Kimberly, you have a girlfriend.*

Kimberly (to Solo): *Well, Solo, I know we've been together and whatever, but I had somebody before you, and I love you and I love her, too.*

Solo (to Kimberly): *I just messed up my whole relationship for you. I messed up everything for you. You want to tell me you're with somebody else?*

Jerry (to Kimberly): *And your other girlfriend doesn't know that? Well, she's been watching backstage, but she didn't know about Solo? Okay, here she is. What's her name? Telly....*

I don't mean to withhold important information, but you probably don't need the Psychic Friends Network to help you figure out what is going to happen next. So, for purposes of expediency, we're going to fast-forward through the next 36 minutes of the program. Unfortunately, that means we won't get to hear Cheryl, Nick, and Shane, or Kim, Lani, and Justin tell their stories. You can consult a tape of Jerry's May 17, 1999, show if you want to find out which of them, if any, end up in emergency care. I would advise you to do this if you are particularly concerned that the recent rash of cheating boyfriends who turn out to be cheating girlfriends may reach epidemic proportions. I would strongly advise you to do this if you're planning to contribute money to a foundation that's fighting the problem.

I can't speak for Jerry, but given his history, I'm sure he would hope you would do just that—open your heart and your wallet. It would gratify his concerned humanitarian side. After all, that is Jerry's motivation for telling us these real-life stories. With their signature style, the talkers bring us close to the "Great Issues of Our Day." They use their excellent training and powerful connections well. They earn their Emmys and high ratings for a reason.

And they prepare us to watch the evening news, which, after all, is just more information about more problems. After an hour with Solo and friends, I feel primed to hear about what's happening in my community and in the world from the mouth of my favorite trusted anchor, confident that no matter how bad it looks, I'm still going to have a better evening than Vixen. It's important to be prepared, because the community and the world usually look pretty bad when my trusted anchor tells the story. Someone once said that if you play a country music song backwards, your love comes home, you get your job back, and your pick-up truck runs again. News reports are the same way: Play them forward and everything seems to be coming apart. But after living in syndication for an hour, how bad can things look? Can the hazards, dangers, troubles, problems, and trials of daily life in our community or our country look as ugly as, say, Jerry's audience?

That's the brilliance of the talkers' contribution. They hand us over to the newsies all ready to feel good about ourselves.

And that poses a monumental challenge to the newsies, who have to stretch pretty far to find anything that will match, "My Boyfriend Is a Woman!"

But, the newsies are clever and they know what's being asked of them. Take a look at how well they rise to the occasion.

Hour Two: Live at Five

(Dead by Six)

5:00:00 PM: TEASE

Your source for news and information..."Eyewitness News"...with Harold Greene; Lisa McRee; Dallas Raines, weather; and Todd Donoho, sports. Now, live ABC/7 "Eyewitness News" at five.

Hi, I'm Larry Kane. Next on "News Three": Angry parents go searching for answers after two students were accused of raping another in a South Philadelphia classroom; the man who killed a women who tape recorded her final moments apologizes to her family; and find out how a former "Annie" plans to get even with Broadway. Now, coverage you can count on. This is KYW "News Three" at five.

Despite desperate attempts to save his life, this diver vanished beneath the treacherous waters of a Livonia dam. Next on Seven, find out what went wrong and how his family is coping. Plus, see how part of your wardrobe may work better than wrinkle cream. Next, on "Action News" at five, where "Seven Stands for News."

Hello, I'm Marc Bailey. And I'm Robin Sewell. "News Fifteen" brings you the local news of the day with live coverage of late-breaking stories on the ground and in the air from Chopper Fifteen. Plus, we give you information that could change your life. It could be as simple as helping thousands of people collect unclaimed money from the state to telling you about diseases that go undetected in women and opening our phone lines with doctors available for you to call for advice. Our no-nonsense approach not only gives you the news, but we offer solutions.

Disembodied Voice: *Only on "News Fifteen." Now, live, local, late-breaking "News Fifteen" at five.*

5:00:30 PM: INVENTING A RIOT

Marc: *The police were out in force today and, tomorrow, they'll be out again.*

Robin: *The plan is to make their presence known near the area of Seventh Street and Roeser to make sure what happened today doesn't happen again. As "News Fifteen"'s Paul Joncich reports, what started out as a fight between two students escalated into...*

Stop the tape. Escalated into what? After some of the unspeakable tragedies that have happened at public schools, I cringe when I think about what's coming next.

Except fortunately, mercifully, nothing much is coming next. There was no violence at this school. There were no fatalities or injuries. This situation is what professionals call a slow news day. That's television talk for no one was bleeding. Which means it's time to make something out of nothing.

Under these circumstances—only under these circumstances—we are treated to the news that what started out as a fight between two students *escalated into a group brawl.*

It's easy to envision pictures of scraped, mud-strewn high school kids mulling around a parking lot over the banner, on-screen headline "Small Scuffle!" But that would defeat the purpose of the story. So the news director opted to play it another way.

Let's see if you think like a news director. The purpose of this story is to:
   a. Give the impression that it bleeds because there is no other lead;
   b. Use pictures of people running around to make people think they're watching a real news story;
   c. Validate the sage advice, "never let the facts get in the way of a good riot."

If you said all of the above you should get your resume ready for our 5:42 PM segment, "You Can Be a News Director."

The telltale sign that something about this story is strange comes in the first line of Paul's report: *It probably looked worse than it was.* Translation: No news here.

Paul: *Dozens of high school students running from police. Officers in riot gear clearing the streets around South Mountain High School after a fight between several students escalated into a rock-throwing melee.*

English translation: What started as an ordinary fight among several students in a matter of moments became—an ordinary fight among several students.

These pictures taken from Chopper Fifteen show at least one student taken into custody after a struggle with police.

Translation: This is our top story because we've got pictures.

Ah, yes, the pictures. Kids running through a field. Kids running across the street. Policemen with clubs and helmets. A student pushed to the ground and handcuffed by three officers. Lots of movement. Enough to bump to second place the discovery of a woman's corpse by a group of mountain bikers. There were no pictures of that.

And the pictures looked convincing. I mean, the police were wearing riot gear—how can you not lead with footage of riot gear?

But the key to this story wasn't just the pictures. It was making the pictures work with the writing and the editing. Imagine if the reporter had said, "A tussle broke out today as police responded to reports of a fistfight at a local school." People would turn to the Home Shopping Network as fast as they could reach for the remote control. A problem like this calls for careful writing and a little imagination.

So, you start with an opening shot of a parent, head in hands, staring at something through an iron fence. It's a great establishing shot, because you assume she must be looking at some sort of commotion. Then, cut to the students dashing through the field while the reporter talks about how they are "running from police." Naturally, that should be followed by lots of pictures of police.

But the police mostly mill around. So, that needs to be followed by an action shot. It's a great place for footage of the arrest. We see a student resist unsuccessfully as the cops pull him away from the door of a green pick-up truck, wrestle him to the ground, force his hands behind his back, and prepare to place him in handcuffs in front of what on the small screen looks to be a swarm of police and students. Next, some audio: shrieks of several dozen students as they run down the street in front of the school. Then we see more police in riot gear patrolling the street, and more parents looking worried.

We need a sound bite. It couldn't have been too difficult to find a student willing to predict future doom: *There's gonna be a lot of trouble tomorrow. They're gonna have guns, knives, and chains and stuff, and they're gonna come to school and have another riot, but worse.*

Well, maybe not. It turns out things were pretty quiet the next day. But the next day is irrelevant to what we're doing now: seamlessly editing pictures, copy, and sound bites into a pretty compelling story with a plot that's far more interesting than what really happened.

Since we react to the pictures more than the words, we may find ourselves thinking, "I hope that kid is wrong, and they don't have another riot at that school tomorrow." So, it's a good time for the reporting crew to remind us again that we didn't quite see what we thought we just saw. It's now time for...

5:02:45 PM: A REASSURING SEGUE

Paul: *It may be important to point out that it was only a few years ago that South Mountain High was rated one of the top high schools in the country. Despite what happened today, school will go on as scheduled tomorrow.*

Robin: *And I think a lot of these kids really have a good attitude, and they don't want what happened today to take away from all the good stuff they do.*

Marc: *They're really proud of their school.*

Paul: *Some of the students say that it looked a lot worse than it was.*

Maybe that could have been the title for the story.

Robin and Marc: *Thanks, Paul.*

5:03:00 PM: ONLY POPULAR RESTAURANTS ARE DANGEROUS

Elsewhere this evening, more news was presented about nothing. But at least this time we get to see footage of an old murder. The anchor is Larry Kane:

Official documents have been released which shed brand new light on the Main Line murder at the General Wayne Inn. Co-owner James Webb was shot to death at the popular historic restaurant last December.

Have you noticed that, regardless of where you live, violence like this only occurs at places that are "popular"? You'll never hear a restaurant crime scene described as "over-rated and lacking charm" or "that place with lousy service." I guess the unpopular places are a lot safer. It must be because they're so empty.

Anyway, I digress. Larry is saying:

Within a few days police searched the home of the restaurant's co-owner, who has not been charged in this case. His lawyer says his client did nothing wrong. But sources tell "News Three" there are questions about the co-owner's whereabouts at the time of the murder. Sources quote him as saying he had drinks with an employee after leaving the inn and then went home. Officials say the employee committed suicide last week because she was reportedly distraught over that relationship.

So, what have we got here? A dead owner and a suspicious co-owner who has not been charged with anything. You might think he was being implicated by Larry Kane, except Larry is careful to tell us the co-owner's lawyer claims his client did nothing wrong.

But what about those vague "questions" about his whereabouts during the murder, raised by equally mysterious "sources"? Or the drinks with an employee who subsequently killed herself? Or the vague nature of their "relationship"?

Well, there has to be some rationale for putting this story near the top of the show, even though no formal charges were filed, and the deaths happened in the past.

And that reason is clear to anyone familiar with the newsies' version of the criminal justice system. On television news, trials are great when you can get them because they look so much like "Law and Order." But you can't always get them, which poses an inconvenience when you're trying to slot something interesting at 5:03 PM.

Fortunately, the newsies can always present select facts from a case just by digging up file footage. It looks and sounds like a trial, but it's better in a way because it can be dredged up on command. And they don't have to worry about other potential inconveniences like the presumption of innocence, because they're not responsible for holding real trials. They can leave those details to real-world jurists like Judge Judy, people who hold in their hands the fates of real defendants.

For us, we've got a great excuse to see murder footage that otherwise would end up wasting away in the archives. And we can draw our own conclusions about what happened at the restaurant.

5:05:50 PM: TEASE

Lisa McRee: *Well, later in this broadcast, scary stories about breast implants haven't stopped the rush to get them. We'll have a special report. And, it can happen at any time, without warning. We'll tell you what it is.*

Dallas Raines: *I'm Dallas Raines. We haven't used those umbrellas in a while, but you may need them—and soon. The forecast is coming up next.*

While local news takes 3 minutes out to pay for itself, we'll take 3 minutes to address a matter that should be foremost on your mind.

One day, you are going to be on television news. I know this because there are so many news programs out there that they're rapidly depleting the available number of real people who can be sources. Just do the math: 260 million Americans divided by—let's take a rough estimate—200 billion news shows. That sort of imbalance can quickly cause a scarcity of crime witnesses and worried neighbors. So, I want you to be prepared when it happens. I don't want you to blow your chance.

There are a couple of things you should know so you're prepared when that microphone is raised to your mouth.

The first is that what you say matters. Nobody ever made it on the air because they weren't worried about uncertainty and danger.

The second is the time it takes to say it matters even more. Anything important can be expressed in less than 4 seconds.

Imagine you're approached by a local news reporter who tells you there was a murder in your neighborhood and the suspect is still at large. She wants to get your reaction for "Live at Five." You agree. She asks you how you feel. You say something like, "Crime is so random that I can't be bothered to torment myself fretting over the possibility that I'll be next."

Wrong answer.

It's not an unreasonable answer. But it's the wrong answer. Skilled reporters are likely to find it to be too measured and rational. Remember, the audience will be looking at you while you talk. And if you look ordinary enough to win the role of scared neighbor, you just won't be as interesting to look at as a bunch of kids running across a street to escape a riot that wasn't happening. Understandably, what you say has to compensate for this lack of action. So, the reporter will need something emotional, something hysterical, something like, "It's scary. This is a quiet neighborhood. Nobody's safe anywhere."

Acceptable responses might also refer to your intention to lower the blinds, bolt the door, keep a weapon by your bed, or shop for enough canned goods so you don't have to leave the house for a month.

Say it in 4 seconds or less, and you're on the air.

Now, you might ask me, "What if I'm not scared, but I still want to be on TV?" If you're thinking this way, it's probably a good time to consider the Fundamental Rule of television: It is a pretend medium. That means it's okay to tell a reporter you're scared even if you aren't, as long as you keep it to 4 seconds. People on television say lots of things they don't mean. Aren't senators on television a lot? I think you see my point.

At this moment, you may feel uncomfortable telling a reporter something you don't believe. Hopefully, this will change by the time you've finished reading this book. For now, you may also be able to take some comfort in knowing that TV news slots are available for real people that don't require you to talk about how you feel. For instance, you could be a witness, or even a near-witness to a news event. Then, all you have to do is talk in sound bites about what you saw, or, if you didn't actually see anything, what you believe you would have seen had you been paying attention. This is an easy role to play, because it just requires following a reporter's lead about what you think happened at a crime, accident, or fire scene.

Here's an example. Anchor Guy Gordon looks resolutely at the camera and says:

The peace of a quiet Oak Park community was shattered tonight by the blast of a shotgun. Two people died in a violent confrontation, and their killer could be someone they both knew. Channel Seven's Kathy Walsh is live at the scene with more. And what are police telling us tonight, Kathy?

When you hear an opening like this, you can bet that sometime in the next 30 seconds you're going to hear from an eyewitness. And that eyewitness can be you.

Kathy: *Guy, police right now are questioning a suspect. They found him here in the victim's front yard when they arrived, and it appears he knew the husband and wife who are the presumed victims.*

You watch as police cordon off the crime scene with yellow tape. Be patient—the eyewitness is on the way. Kathy stops talking to Guy and now addresses the audience directly:

Several shots rang out tonight in this normally quiet Oak Park neighborhood. The sound caught Herbert Finkel's attention.

Five seconds into the story and we're ready to cue Herbert Finkel. He's the neighbor from Central Casting, a pleasant middle-aged man with an authentic look, which is valuable, because it keeps the audience from confusing him with Guy Gordon. Good reporters know neighbors have to look like what the public expects.

Now, anyone schooled in how to make news judgments knows that Finkel is about to say he heard a loud explosion. They know this because Kathy Walsh has already used the terms "shotgun blast" and "caught Herbert Finkel's attention." The missing piece is the loud noise. If you looked in a local reporter's *How to Construct a Story* manual, under "Noises, Loud: Shotgun Blasts," you would find the entry: "Shotgun blasts not captured on videotape must be confirmed within seconds of their mention by a witness attesting to a loud noise. The witness should preferably look like a typical neighbor (see Finkel, Herbert)."

Finkel looks past the camera and says, *I saw a man coming out of the doorway across the street from me and it looked like he had, like, a shotgun. And*—here it comes—*I heard a bang, and then I saw him run back into the house again, and he came back out again, and*—it's worth repeating—*another bang.*

Two bangs in one sound bite. Total time: 6 seconds. That's very long for an ordinary piece, so Kathy needs to justify the extra exposure she's awarded to Herbert Finkel by demonstrating that this is an unusually important story. Under the circumstances, a second witness is in order.

Kathy: *So, Herbert called 911. So did Diane Powell, who not only heard the shots but saw the person who may have fired them.*

At this point, Walsh plays detective. She already has a witness attesting to the crime. Now, she needs someone to validate Finkel's reaction. This is where Diane Powell comes in. Showing off reporting skills no doubt honed during a career spent at similar crime scenes, Kathy refers to the person Diane saw running from the scene and asks her:

Do you think he's the one who did it?

Let's stop to consider the various things Diane could say. "I have no idea, Kathy. It was dark. He could have been making a pizza delivery."

That's honest, but not interesting. If Diane Powell said this, she would be forgetting the Fundamental Rule.

She could say, "I'm not going to presume anything, Kathy. People in this country are innocent until proven guilty. I would hate to implicate somebody because of what could be no more than a coincidence of timing. If I were wrong, it might amount to little more than a small injustice. But small injustices add up, and collectively they can undermine the social fabric of our nation."

That's got a righteous tone, but it sounds a little high and mighty. And it's much too long.

If you want to be on television, there's only one answer to this question: "I assume he did." It's brief, understandable, commonsensical, and did I mention that it's brief?

Diane looks at Kathy. She says:

I assume he did.

Diane Powell understood the Fundamental Rule.

5:09:00 PM: FEELING THE BAROMETRIC PRESSURE

We're back, and it's time to check the weather for the first time. I have to confess that there's a lot I don't really understand about weather reports. What most people need to know about the weather can be determined by looking out the window.

But people seem to love weather reports. Lots of people tune in local news primarily to get the weather. They just put up with the stuff about the murders in popular restaurants while they're waiting.

This creates a problem for the newsies. On one hand, if viewers are looking for weather, they'll expect a real show—weather in capital letters. On the other hand, most weather reports can be boiled down to this:

"It's hot today. Sunny, too. It won't be tonight, though. Back to you."

The problem is you can say it all in 4 seconds. This, of course, normally would be an asset. But, because weather reports are so inherently entertaining, they're the one place where the brevity clause in the Fundamental Rule doesn't apply. In fact, weather reports draw such a large audience that they need to be drawn out as much as possible and repeated throughout the show. Enter the Weather Corollary to the Fundamental Rule: Successful weather reports should contain as much extraneous information as possible.

Everything else on a local news program is linked to your home town—it's what news directors call the "Local Angle." The weather is the lone exception. One of the first things you'll hear from a weather reporter ("meteorologist" if the station has a big budget, "weather expert" if it does not) is about weather conditions in some remote part of the country:

"There's a big ridge of high pressure slowly moving through the western Great Lakes, bringing fair weather to the upper peninsula of Michigan, while a cold front over the central plains is colliding with warm, moist air from the Gulf, bringing heavy showers and thunderstorms to a region stretching from western Louisiana all the way up the Mississippi valley to southern Illinois."

I would be pleased to know this if I lived in any of these places. But if I lived in any of these places, I would be hearing about the trough in the jet stream that's bringing unseasonably cool weather to New England.

No matter where I live, I'm bound to get the forecast for places where I don't live in language straight out of a meteorology course. Weather segments are the only place where they try to keep things complicated. So we hear about "fronts" and "systems" when a simple "it's raining out" would suffice. This complexity would only pose a problem for news directors, though, if the point of weather reports was actually to communicate information about the weather.

Weather is such a big deal that many stations invest a lot of money to make their reports as convincing as possible. One of the most impressive techniques is a three-dimensional computer simulation of satellite photos that allows you to travel under and around the clouds like you're on a big weather roller coaster. Maybe you've seen it. Large chunks of the country whisk by below you and big H's and L's float off to the side as clouds appear and disappear from above. In an effort to emphasize the storms, the computer program usually sets off rain clouds in a distinct color, such as light green. It's a bit disconcerting, actually. I don't know about you, but I don't want anything light green falling from the sky.

Even when they get around to the main event, it's dressed up with meteorological minutiae that you probably don't need to know: "The barometer reads 30.02 inches, and it's falling." How often have you used that information to check the accuracy of the barometer that you have hanging on your living room wall? "The record low for this date was 10 degrees, set back in 1889." I remember it well.

So, everything about the weather is backwards. Unlike the rest of "Live at Five," it's neither local nor simple. Complexity is a virtue, and brevity is a vice. Sometimes, it just doesn't make any sense at all. I mean, exactly why is it news that it snowed in the winter? Isn't it supposed to snow in the winter?

5:11:45 PM: WHAT EVER HAPPENED TO THE STORY ABOUT THE BREAST IMPLANTS?

Be patient. And expect that the tease will be repeated at least two and possibly three more times before the actual story is aired. It follows directly from the Fundamental Rule:

Fundamental Rule Postulate 26: When constructing a newscast, try to use the term "breast implants" as frequently as possible.

5:12:00 PM: MOVIE—OR REALITY?

For 5 seconds the nonstop sound of bullets firing fills your living room. You watch a stoic police car block an empty street, set off against the backdrop of the Hollywood hills. The banner on-screen headline screams "Terror in the Streets." All this may be happening in another city, but with so much violent footage available to your local station, it must be important news. Guy Gordon essentially tells you as much:

That is the echo of rapid-fire rage in Los Angeles, the aftermath of a botched robbery. Gunmen dressed and armed to kill turn a neighborhood into a battlefield with police. And the question lingers—did any of the bad guys get away?

When the bullets stopped flying, two robbers were dead. Tonight, police aren't sure if others may be on the run after this Hollywood shootout.

The scene changes to a man in body armor crouched behind a car shooting an assault rifle in the air. The headline now says "Hollywood Shootout."

Channel Seven's Mike Huckman is in the satellite center with incredible videotape of this very real drama.

It's no wonder Guy is emphasizing that this was a real drama, because the pictures that follow look like something out of fiction. There's a tight shot of a man in dark glasses spraying automatic bullets across cars on a busy street. Police hiding behind a U-Haul truck return fire. Bystanders in a plaza run in all directions. A man in a car aims a rifle out the window and fires into a crowd. Inside the bank, a man in a ski mask, his face covered by a scarf, aims a weapon at an unarmed bank guard, who crouches on his knees and puts his hands behind his head. Back on the street, a well-dressed detective type resembling Al Pacino exchanges gunfire with one of the suspects.

Come to think of it, that is Al Pacino. On the news? In the middle of Guy Gordon's real-life drama?

The on-screen headline now says "Real Life Rampage." Mike Huckman has just finished telling us: *TV viewers in Los Angeles today watched two fatal shootouts unfold right before their eyes— live. It wasn't a violent TV show or some Hollywood shoot-em-up. It was real.*

Perhaps. But what we're watching comes right off the three-day rental shelf at the video store. It's footage depicting a robbery of the sort that happened today in Hollywood, lifted from the Hollywood film, "Heat." Mike clarifies things for us:

It may sound cliché, but it was like a scene out of a movie. "Heat," to be specific, the 1995 film starring Al Pacino in which a bunch of bandits hold up a downtown Los Angeles bank and get in a shootout in traffic. The only difference is this happened at a suburban North Hollywood bank.

It all goes by so quickly that you need a minute to sort it out. First, we're watching footage of a real gun battle over the headline "Hollywood Shootout," which brings to mind footage from a movie. Then, we're watching footage of a fake gun battle from a movie over the headline, "Real-Life Rampage." So which is it?

If you say the answer to this question is "Does it really matter?" you're beginning to appreciate the full impact of the Fundamental

Rule. Guy and Mike have presented us with an ingenious way of appreciating the nuances of this news item by using an art form we're all familiar with—fake R-rated violence—to establish a frame of reference for the story. This time, there was more than enough real action footage to justify placing the story toward the beginning of "Live at Five." Guy and Mike didn't have to use clips from the film as filler or to simulate what really happened.

But, they were shrewd enough to recognize that morphing real footage with movie footage made the story more believable by making everything seem staged. Who better than Al Pacino to lend legitimacy to a news item about a gun fight between police and "bad guys," as Guy put it. As in the movies, this battle ended with a number of police and innocent civilians wounded but alive and the two suspects dead. The fact that it all happened in Hollywood was a stroke of luck that tied everything together. The resulting piece is better than a simple news story. It plays like a 3-minute coming attractions reel for an action-adventure flick, opening this summer in theatres everywhere. When it comes to news reporting, you simply can't do it any better than that.

5:15:00 PM: THE GREAT BAKING POWDER INCIDENT

How do you follow a story like the "Hollywood Shootout?" You could air details of the package in a pick-up truck that FBI agents are examining to make sure it doesn't contain explosives destined for a terrorist bombing. At this point, there's plenty of reason to believe the package is harmless, but considering the anniversaries of the Branch Davidian raid and the Oklahoma City bombing loom on the horizon, it's best to take a look, just for good measure.

You could write the story like this:

"Authorities in Texas are looking for two men in a U-Haul truck containing a package believed to be harmless but which could contain explosives. Their motives are unknown, but terrorist threats surrounding the anniversaries of the Branch Davidian raid and the Oklahoma City bombing are motivating FBI agents to find the

U-Haul truck in the event it contains a bomb. Authorities emphasize this is a routine investigation, and acknowledge it is likely to pose no reason for concern."

You could report this over a graphic of a U-Haul truck with the banner headline, "No Reason for Concern."

If you did, you would never make it in television. You could try out in markets so small that the news team personally knows all the victims it covers—markets too small to have popular restaurants—and you still wouldn't get work. If your instincts told you to write the story this way, I would strongly recommend you consult the 5:16:15 PM segment, "You Can Be a Newswriter." Realistically, after sitting through a great preview for an Al Pacino movie, why would anyone want to hear about an out-of-town U-Haul truck that no one is worried about?

Fortunately, there's a way to take the same material and make it newsworthy. Here's how a pro would do it.

The opening graphic would say, "Terrorist Threat." An artist's sketch of a somber, serious, middle-aged white male would appear on the screen. Guy would advise us to lock our doors:

If the FBI gets its way, the man in this police composite will have nowhere to hide. Investigators believe he may have explosive intentions and is trying to find him before it's too late. The FBI fear a gas station fill-up, a U-Haul truck, and the load it is carrying may be a dangerous combination that adds up to a powerful bomb.

Tell the audience that fifty U.S. Bureau of Alcohol, Tobacco, and Firearms agents are on the trail of the suspect in the drawing. Only then raise the possibility that there may be nothing here:

At the same time, there is the possibility this could all be a big misunderstanding.

But be sure to temper your reassurance with the appropriate level of fear. What if it isn't a big misunderstanding? Offer this quote from a law enforcement official: *If it isn't a big misunderstanding, we've got something to worry about here.* Address the *highly credible* reasons why authorities are worried. Mention that the suspects appear suspicious (Fundamental Rule Postulate 14: Suspects always look suspicious. That's what makes them suspects). Say that they were seen filling containers with diesel fuel at a gas station near Fort Worth, Texas, while the cargo area of their truck *seemed to be loaded with more than two tons of ammonium nitrate fertilizer, the same stuff used to blow up the Oklahoma City federal building.*

It's not necessary to say who thought it seemed to be filled with explosives, or even why.

Add, *another witness says there were wires in the truck, possible detonators.* That helps elevate the speculation to a higher level. Then, deftly downplay the fear angle once again by saying authorities investigating the matter *believe the men could be farmers who bought the stuff for a very innocent use.* It's okay; the audience is already too worried to recognize this as a rational statement. And you can subsequently defend your story as balanced and reasonable.

At the same time, you haven't lost sight of your mission to find hysteria where others find concern. Hysteria is: "Excessive or uncontrollable fear or other strong emotion." Concern is: "A matter that relates to or affects one; something of interest or importance." Authorities are concerned. They might even be relieved if the material in the truck didn't turn out to be explosives.

Concern doesn't keep people tuned in for the 5:16 PM denture adhesive ads.

It turns out that the alarm raised by this story was false. By the next day, FBI officials were reporting that the material in the U-Haul truck was baking powder. It's not clear why these two suspects were transporting two tons of baking powder. Maybe they were going to make a big pastry. In any event, the only danger they posed to society was the threat that the hot Texas sun would leaven their truck.

What do you do now? It's tempting to drop the story completely and let a hint of uncertainty hang in the air. Drawing attention to a follow-up piece is certainly out of the question, because there's no good way to feature a story where the word "dud" appears in the lead. A good compromise is to bury the follow-up in a quick blurb strategically placed right before a weather update, deep in the next day's newscast. It would sound something like this:

The FBI has dropped a nationwide terrorist threat advisory after a U-Haul truck suspected of carrying the makings of a huge bomb turned out to be a dud.

Here are a few stories you might consider airing first, taken directly from the newscast where the follow-up appeared:

- *Anger and outrage in Westland, where people who had to clean up raw sewage from their basements last week say they're fed up* (there's an important local angle here);
- A feces-infested "Hell House" in Lansing, Michigan (it was an unusually big news day for excrement);
- An "in-depth" interview with comedian Tim Allen;

and seven other stories. Perhaps there were no terrorists, but that shouldn't prevent good reporters from blowing up our concerns.

5:15:52 PM: TEASE

Harold: *Coming up here just a little later, the story of a woman fighting for the right to wear pants at work. And, it could happen on any flight, without warning. It's terrifying turbulence, and it can cause serious harm. Tonight, "Action News" reveals how it happens and how to protect yourself in a story you'll see only on Seven.*

Lisa: *Also, Laura Diaz looks at some of the concerns raised by the latest rush to get breast implants in her special report.*

5:16:00 PM: PROMO

I feel a little badly about that last comment about blowing up our concerns. It demonstrated insensitivity to the pressure the newsies are under to hold your attention. You have to figure that they're just keeping pace with the talkers.

And the talkers are dropping their brand of speculation right into the middle of "Live at Five." Just look at this promo that forms the bridge between the baking powder story and the denture adhesive ads:

Deep Disembodied Voice: *Ahead, on "Hard Copy": Make your waiter mad and you may pay. We discovered some restaurants' dirty little secrets.*

Woman's Voice: *People spit in people's salads.*

Deep Disembodied Voice: *A Special Report: recipe for revenge. Are air bags taking a back seat to safety? They're supposed to save lives, but some say they're child killers.*

Woman's Voice: *Imagine having a child decapitated.*

Deep Disembodied Voice: *The scare bag scandal. And—Michael Jackson's mask may be his best move yet. We exposed where dangerous dirty germs are growing, and how they can attack you in a phone booth or a bank machine. Life under the microscope, on "Hard Copy."*

By this point, the mental picture produced by imagining a couple of would-be terrorists on the loose doesn't seem so bad.

5:16:15 PM: AD TIME-OUT: YOU CAN BE A NEWSWRITER

Those promos were so distressing, we might be best served by skipping the rest of the ads in this break and devoting 4 minutes to something even more important than attack germs waiting to ambush you as you innocently dial a public phone. Let's take a quick look at the skills you'll need to become part of the forgotten underbelly of television news. That's right—with a little coaching, you could qualify to be a television newswriter before the next weather report. This could be your chance to live sequentially in a series of small, out-of-the-way cities for weeks at a time while earning perhaps as much as minimum wage. All it takes is a flair for adjectives, the ability to condense a lot of information into a few words, and knowledge of the formula.

What makes newswriting so easy to do once you learn the basics is that most of the stories you'll write are stories you've written before. Of course, the particulars change—the names, places, and such. But that's not important. Apart from the details of who was murdered and who committed the crime, the restaurant killing on Philadelphia's Main Line could have happened in Detroit; the shooting in suburban Oak Park, Michigan, observed by neighbor Herbert Finkel might well have been in Phoenix; and the school riot that didn't happen in Phoenix could just as easily not have happened anywhere else. The "Hollywood Shootout" was on the local news everywhere, thanks to shared video of the event, even though it was only a local story in L.A.

This provides a bonanza for the newswriter, because she can traverse the country as she changes jobs without ever having to learn anything about the local community where she is presently employed. All she has to do is rely on the formula.

You start by writing a lead-in that the anchor will read to introduce the story. It should condense the important facts of the story into a sentence or two, embellished with ear-catching phrases. You should describe the victim—as "desperate," "cut down in his prime," "tragically in the wrong place at the wrong time," or whatever selection strikes you as interesting as you glance through your newswriter's bible, the *Thesaurus of Clichés and Aphorisms*. You need to do it in a way that will evoke a reaction from the viewer, preferably fear, anger, fear, disgust—perhaps fear.

But, you won't need to work too hard on this part of your story because it will be delivered by the anchor, who will embellish whatever you write with his brand of prose, designed to compliment his fine performance skills. Good anchors get viewers to react to the words of writers, which is why they are widely referred to as "the talent" and live so much higher on television's food chain. Really good anchors can cry on command. The exceptional ones get weepy at civic events talking about the bond they feel with the people of the city where they work. The extraordinary ones can name the city.

Once you've written the opening to the story, you need a good follow-through. This is where the formula comes in. Learn it and you will never be hungry again, once you learn to live on beans.

Let's play a game. I'll give you seven lists of phrases, and you can write your own lead local story, just like a professional newswriter. It's easy—and it's fun. Each list gives you five choices of things like crime scenes, victims, and so forth. Just mix and match your favorites, making one selection from each list, and you're ready for air:

List 1

Downtown tonight,
In a crime-riddled neighborhood this evening,
On a typically quiet street, moments ago,
In a peaceful rural setting earlier today,
In broad daylight today,

List 2

two
five
twenty
hundreds of
countless numbers of

List 3

children
homeless persons
senior citizens
teenagers
families

List 4

were found
were reported missing and are presumed to have been

according to unnamed sources were
reportedly were
appear to have been

List 5

fatally
critically
savagely
brutally
inexplicably

List 6

shot
beaten
stabbed
assaulted
burned

List 7

in a tragic incident eyewitnesses are calling nothing short of gruesome.
in a tragic incident eyewitnesses are calling nothing short of gruesome.
in a tragic incident eyewitnesses are calling nothing short of gruesome.
in a tragic incident eyewitnesses are calling nothing short of gruesome.
in a tragic incident eyewitnesses are calling nothing short of gruesome.

Just consider the possibilities. One day, you can write this story: "On a typically quiet street, moments ago, hundreds of homeless persons were found savagely beaten in a tragic incident eyewitnesses are calling nothing short of gruesome." You can follow it up with: "In broad daylight today, two teenagers appear to have been brutally assaulted, in a tragic incident eyewitnesses are calling nothing short of gruesome." These lists provide you with enough story possibilities to last between six and eight weeks, at which point you should be well on your way to another city, where you can start again.

Once you get the hang of the formula, it's easy to imagine yourself one day becoming a producer or news director and constructing the rest of the story. You'll need a grainy photo of at least one victim, preferably taken during happier times if you're into ironic contrast. Don't forget the eyewitnesses, and be sure they say something about a loud noise. Police in uniform are optional but desirable for authenticity. You can count on them to use words like "perpetrator" and "suspect." If you can't get an artist's rendering of the alleged bad guy, any rendering of any scowling person will do (remember smiling pictures of bad guys rub audiences the wrong way).

Blood or the promise of blood is a must, so if there are no bodies available, do the best you can, even if that only means showing yellow crime scene tape that says "Police Line: Do Not Cross." Whenever appropriate, toss in an interview with shocked neighbors of the accused, who will tell you how baffled they are to learn they were living next to a homicidal maniac. (Fundamental Rule Postulate 5: Homicidal maniacs are only credible if a neighbor testifies to their apparent normalcy by saying, "He always kept to himself and was always so polite." Postal Worker Exception to Fundamental Rule Postulate 5: When the homicide occurs in a post office, credibility is best preserved by omitting the "polite" part.)

Practice it. With very little effort, you'll be in Thunder Bay before you know it, saying you had no idea work could be this easy.

5:20:00 PM: FIRST FEATURE: IT COULD HAPPEN ANY TIME WITHOUT WARNING

Now that you've had your first contact with newswriting essentials, let's see how well you can do writing a feature story. Keep in mind, I'm starting you off with an important assignment. Feature stories always get a wonderful build-up. Sometimes they're teased throughout the day on ads for the evening's broadcast. For some viewers, they're the reason for tuning in today. This great hype potential makes them ideal for any newscast. And producers love them because, unlike stories built around actual news events, they can be planned, written, and compiled well in advance. Feature stories preclude that nasty waiting until the last minute that's such an unappealing part of reporting real news.

The story you're going to write is about something that can happen at any time, without warning. Maybe you remember that this piece was teased 4 minutes ago as a story "you'll see only on Seven." Go back to 5:15:52—it's there. That should have been the giveaway that it's a feature piece. Think about how silly it would be for a news anchor to say that a crime story will be heard only on his station, as if any one station had an exclusive working relationship with the police department. On the other hand, Channel Seven knew that no other station would do this story because there is no news in it for the others to cover. Management could be confident that the competition would be busy running *different* stories with no news in them.

So, here's your challenge: Take a story that's not built around a news event, that has been hyped all day, and that may be the primary reason some in your audience are watching. Using everything you learned about being a newswriter, find a way to make the story pay off.

To do this successfully, you'll need to identify your strengths. First, find an emotional angle to the story. The thing that can happen any time, without warning, is turbulence on an aircraft, something many travelers will admit can make them feel shaken or a little out of control. All aircraft experience turbulence, of course, and are designed to withstand it; basically it's a condition of flying that at some point you will experience turbulence on an aircraft, most likely during meal and beverage service. If you think of turbulence this way, as simply a commonplace event that happens all the time, it has no news value. But, if you think of it as a commonplace event that many people never get used to, it has great news value. More precisely, the way people react to it has great news value.

You should easily be able to identify the emotional space where this story fits. It has to evoke apprehension, anxiety, and fear, playing on that part of us that feels it requires a leap of faith to leave the ground and travel 500 miles per hour in an aluminum tube. Your choice of adjectives will determine just how well you can convey this. Will you succumb to the temptation to say at some point, "the sky is falling"?

Next, draw on pictures that reinforce these feelings. The seed for this feature came from a story that happened a few weeks earlier when an airliner had to make an emergency landing in another city after unusually severe turbulence injured some people on board. You'll be able to use footage of injured people being carried off that plane to emphasize your point. Make sure you choose shots of ordinary-looking people, using the same principle we apply when we select next-door neighbors. You want viewers thinking, "That could be me."

The real challenge is putting all this together in a piece that frightens without being unreasonable. If you tell people they *will* encounter dangerous turbulence, their experiences will contradict your words and they won't believe you. Our audience isn't stupid—people know that most flights work out just fine. Instead, tell them how they *could* experience dangerous turbulence. You know, the next flight you take *could* be a rocky one with painful consequences. That's a statement people can accept. Lot's of things *could* happen. And, claiming something could happen frees you from the inconvenience of having to show that it will.

Just like the stories of the nonriot and the nonbomb, be careful to remind the audience periodically that things are not as bad as they seem. Just do it in a way that doesn't reassure too much. It's best to alternate calm, reasonable statements with scary, provocative ones, like this:

Disembodied Voice (over ominous music): *And now...Special Assignment...*(I don't know what a "Special Assignment" is, but it really makes the story seem important.)

Guy: *It's been compared to potholes in the sky* (scary, provocative). *Turbulence is often nothing more than a minor bump in flight* (calm, reasonable), *but there are some times when it can take you on a rollercoaster ride at 30,000 feet* (scary, provocative). *Veteran flyers insist* *that it's nothing to be afraid of because planes are designed to take that kind of punishment* (calm, reasonable). *But that's little comfort when you're being tossed around the cabin in a pocket of terrifying turbulence* (scary, provocative).

Cue the footage: A graphic depicting the words "Special Assignment" (you really can't say it too much) fades to pictures of a jetliner sitting in the dark, someone on a stretcher being carried through the night to an ambulance, and a man with a neck brace moving gingerly through an airport. It's time for a long, scary section. You hear the voices of passengers who had unnerving encounters with turbulence:

Female Voice: *For a good 5 to 10 minutes, people were just fearing for their lives.*

Guy: *It can strike with little or no warning.*

Male Voice: *It was definitely scary enough to shake up a bunch of people and make everybody a little bit shaky the whole way here.*

Guy: *The American Airlines flight suddenly dropped hundreds of feet in the air.*

Female Voice: *Food and drinks and everything went everywhere, all over the aisles and all over the people.*

Guy: *The frightening plunge injured ten passengers, most of them seriously enough to force an emergency landing in San Francisco.*

Injured Man (looking fairly healthy): *It would be like me sitting right here, right now, and all of a sudden somebody slammed us into the ceiling twice in less than a second.*

Guy: *He was one of more than a dozen passengers injured when another plane got roughed up at 24,000 feet before landing in Salt Lake City.*

Time to pull back briefly from the edge. We see an airplane taking off normally on a sunny day. Guy assures us, *Most flights manage to avoid turbulence that causes that kind of trouble...*

But?

…but when you're soaring into the wild blue yonder, one stiff jolt can make it feel like (quickly consult the *Thesaurus of Clichés and Aphorisms*) *the sky is falling.* There, he said it.

Reassurance from a Pilot: *You'll see people in the back that are pretty terrified, but there's really no need to be. It feels a lot worse than it is.*

And from a Flight Attendant: *Some cases you are aware that there are some rocky places that you'll climb through. But then sometimes it just happens out of the blue.*

An aviation professor says something about friction and air masses in an attempt to explain the causes of air turbulence in 4 seconds. But, you probably don't hear what he's saying because the Special Assignment people have cooked up a nifty special effect on their computers to keep you interested in the story. You see grainy, black-and-white pictures of an airplane cabin jerking up and down on the screen to simulate turbulence. Whatever reassurance you felt from the pilot and the flight attendant is subtly undermined. So, time for Guy to re-assure us again:

Advanced radar systems usually give pilots enough warning to steer clear of severe conditions…

But?

…but no plane is immune from turbulence, not even Air Force One. We see a picture of the president walking away from the plane. *Thunderstorms tossed it around on a flight to South Carolina last year, leaving the jumbo jet in shambles.* This is unnerving: You can twice carry the electoral votes of California, but it will not offer you protection from terrifying turbulence.

Worse, *there can also be unexpected hits at cruising altitudes, even when it appears to be smooth sailing.* The professor is back, doing a 4-second seminar on clear air turbulence. There are no nifty graphics this time, but he's demonstrating his point by bouncing a small plastic model of a Lufthansa jet, so there's something to hold our interest.

In his honor, perhaps we could stop the tape here and summarize what we've learned:

Turbulence can be scary. Dangerous, too, although chances are you'll never be on a flight where you're at risk of injury.

Since most of us already know this, and since most news producers know most of us already know this, we need to find a way to justify having spent almost 4 minutes of news time on pictures of bouncing planes and accident victims. Otherwise, it might appear that the entire point of the story was to spend almost 4 minutes of news time on pictures of bouncing planes and accident victims.

We need a public service message. How about this:

Guy: *It seems obvious but too few of us actually do it. All the experts we talk to say the best thing you can do to avoid being hurt on a turbulent flight is to just keep that seat belt fastened at all times.*

I think now we know why this was a Special Report.

5:23:30 PM: SEGUE INTO TERRIFYING WEATHER

Diana: *Thank you, Guy. Expect more puddles. The rain we've had all day isn't expected to stop anytime soon, and that could create a problem with flooding. "Action News" science editor Jerry Hodak is here to tell us how much rain to expect, and when we can get some relief. Jerry, everyone's asking, are we going to expect problems from all the rain?*

Jerry: *I don't think there will be any serious problems, no.*

5:24:00 PM: AIR QUALITY

Besides, the rain could help to clear the air and make the air quality acceptable again. Air quality is a favorite but puzzling feature of some weather reports.

Just what are we supposed to do on days when the air quality is unacceptable?

Because so many people watch local news for the weather, being a weathercaster is one of the most important jobs on the air. Not surprisingly, it takes a lot of talent to report the weather effectively, so if you're thinking about trying it yourself you should pay close attention.

There are two types of weathercasters—the scientific type and the artistic type. You can decide which best describes you.

The scientific type consists of people with some sort of training. It may not be in anything related to the weather, but one of the nice things about the flexibility afforded by television is that you are not eliminated from consideration if you happen to be a meteorologist. Producers love to see their anchors introduce the weather by saying, "now here's meteorologist Bill Flatley with the forecast." It lends an enormous amount of credibility to their report, and sort of makes people feel like they're watching someone who has spent the whole day carefully studying weather maps to determine the right forecast.

You get the same credibility with the title *doctor,* which is why scientific-type weather people don't have to be meteorologists as long as they have some credential that allows them to use the title. "Now here's Dr. Bill Flatley with the forecast." The kind of training that produced the degree is far less important than the title itself, although most producers would agree that it would be bad taste to include people with no formal training who've received an honorary degree somewhere. Otherwise, the particulars of the degree are unimportant. Optometrists, take note.

Of course, you get the greatest impact with someone who has a Ph.D. in meteorology. "Now here's meteorologist Dr. Bill Flatley with the forecast." Now *that's* impressive.

And it's not impressive just because of how it sounds. Scientific types really are impressive. The meteorologists understand things like isobars and dew points, things other weathercasters may allude to but about which they have no real understanding. Ask a weathercaster who's not a meteorologist how you can have a relative humidity reading of 100 percent without being entirely under water, and see if you get a convincing answer. The scientific types without meteorological training are impressive, too. Even the optometrists can accurately fit you for contacts.

Since I haven't done a formal survey, I couldn't tell you if most meteorologists are scientific types, but I have a hunch they aren't. The title doesn't come for free, so many smaller market stations can't afford to buy the prestige that science brings. Other stations simply see no need for it, because they can find everything they need in an artistic type.

Weathercasters of the artistic variety need not have formal schooling. Instead, they are adept at communicating their deep, abiding commitment to the weather. They may not be versed in the mathematics of relative humidity, but when they give the reading you know they care. They exude confidence and develop a loyal following, some of whom will not reach for an umbrella without first tuning them in.

In truth, scientific types need to have a little of the artisan in them to succeed, just as artistic types need some basic familiarity with the weather to be convincing. At the very least they have to know how to read a thermometer. If they cannot, their passion for forecasting will appear hollow.

This is more true today than it was in the past because there is an entire cable network devoted to around-the-clock weather forecasting, a network that has taken the concept of weather reports to another level. Where your local station is busy giving you the forecast for other places in the country where you don't live, the cable station is giving you the forecast for parts of the world you may never see. *It looks like another hot one in Bahrain.* Even the least scientific weathercasters now need to compete with this.

Whether scientific or artistic, the successful weathercaster has a clear sense of a weather report's fundamentals. If you want to succeed as a weathercaster, you will need to understand and master the three kinds of weather reports: good weather, annoying weather, and dangerous weather. And you will have to learn how to look at a blank screen and pretend it contains a weather map. Do these two things and you have a future in the business.

Good weather is the hardest to handle. You're going to appear anywhere from two to five times during a typical "Live at Five" program, doing weather spots that range from brief recaps to detailed (3-minute) segments. If all you have to work with is "it's sunny and beautiful today," you can lose your audience fast. You'll have to learn how to draw out your report, how to fill it in with extraneous details. You may spend your afternoon rummaging through footage from parts of the country where they're having hail storms, or play up "trends" in the forecast that suggest "it may be beautiful now but a big change is on the way." People love experiencing good weather, but there's nothing inherently interesting about a good forecast.

Annoying weather is another story. People want to know if they're going to have to walk through puddles or drive through slush. They want the details of how much it's going to rain or when the fog is going to lift. Annoying weather presents weathercasters with the opportunity to shine.

But it poses a different sort of challenge, which is the tendency for news directors to insist as a matter of policy that annoying weather be covered as dangerous weather. We all know what dangerous weather is. Hurricanes and blizzards are dangerous, and they always lead the news regardless of what else is happening. Unfortunately for news directors, most weather conditions are not life-threatening, which means they are not entertaining. Because news directors are the policy arm of the Fundamental Rule, responsible for finding successful ways to pretend, they will readily instruct their weathercasters to issue warnings about conditions that are really more annoying than dangerous. Good weathercasters do it with aplomb.

"Some road surfaces are already starting to become slick, especially on overpasses and in higher elevations, so, please, use good judgment and drive only if it is absolutely necessary."

It's a hard warning to resist, especially when it comes from a doctor/meteorologist, although savvy viewers know that these are generally the best times to venture outside because the roadways are so empty.

Once you have learned how to say the phrase "please, use good judgment" with the proper degree of care and concern, you're ready to work on the most physically demanding part of your job, the part that requires you to look at the audience while pointing to places on a nonexistent weather map. Typically, weathercasters stand in front of a blank, wall-size blue or green screen, on which maps and weather information appears when you're watching at home. Viewers get to see the maps, but weathercasters see only the blank wall. The weathercaster gets to see what the viewer sees from a monitor off the set. At the same time, she has to look at the camera. If you think this is easy, try doing it while little H's and L's float all over the place. Weather doesn't stand still for anybody.

It helps to have a general appreciation for geography, too, because it looks pretty silly if you're talking about Kansas while you're pointing to Kentucky. This is particularly true if you happen to be reporting the weather in Kansas or Kentucky.

When you get right down to it, the real expertise you'll need for your job lies in authoritatively translating information from the blank blue wall to the folks at home. If you can do this, whether you're a scientific type or an artistic type you will be a successful weathercaster. You may want to give it a try at home before auditioning, but the nice thing about being an aspiring weathercaster is you can always fall back on your scientific or artistic skills if things don't work out.

5:29:00 PM: DESSERT

After 29 minutes of relentless emotional prodding, we can use a break before facing more chaos, disaster, and risk. News directors realize this, and often as a matter of policy require a light or even upbeat story at the close of the half-hour, before returning to the reality of terrifying turbulence and terrorists with baking products. The principle is something like satisfying the craving for a sweet dessert after a heavy meal.

During the first 29 minutes, rest assured that animals will appear on the news only if their lives are in danger. During dessert, animals are cuddly:

A zoo in New York has a new addition—a pint-sized pachyderm that packs a punch. This couldn't have been an easy birth. The baby elephant weighed in at 293 pounds, and the mom looks very excited. The new arrival is being called Molly.

Seattle's aquarium is celebrating its twentieth birthday with an added attraction: two new sea otters. An eight-year-old female that was rescued from the Valdez oil spill in Alaska is being loaned by the Tacoma zoo. An eight-year-old male will arrive next month from Sea World in San Diego.

During the first 29 minutes, spirits are down, injuries are horrific, and communities are in disarray. During dessert, the spirits of the injured and disabled are lifted through community action and togetherness, and—although it pushes the boundaries of what's acceptable to say on the air—dreams can even come true.

Mickey Mouse has made his mark in some local kids whose dreams came true today. These are the happy faces of the kids from St. Lucy's Day Care in Upper Darby who returned just an hour ago from Disney World in Florida. Sixteen visually impaired kids got to take a day trip to Disney. Their trip was sponsored by the Great Sunshine Foundation, which has fulfilled the wishes of more than 22,000 handicapped and ill children.

Members of the Phantoms hockey team helped raise the spirits of a severely injured high school wrestler, who was paralyzed in an accident during a practice session. The team is hosting a fund-raiser for the boy, and that will be next month.

We know what happens in restaurants when they lead the news. During dessert, restaurants are transformed into places people go for—dessert.

It was time to tango in Philadelphia tonight at a dinner that honors Argentina. The tango took over the Restaurante Volare on Main Street in Manayunk. The owner of the restaurant is an Italian native who grew up in Argentina. He hosted a classic Argentine dinner to bring the taste and tango of his country to Philadelphia.

We see people dancing, smiling, and generally having a good time. Come to think of it, the restaurant looks pretty crowded. If this weren't the last minute of the newscast, I'd be worried.

5:30:00 PM: HOW MANY TIMES CAN ONE CAR SMASH INTO A HOUSE?

Your source for news and information—"Eyewitness News," with Harold Greene; Lisa McRee; Dallas Raines, weather; and Todd Donoho, sports. Now, live, ABC/7 "Eyewitness News" at Five continues.

Lisa: *A Carson family gets an unwelcome visitor. This was the result when a chase by sheriff's deputies came to a very abrupt end. And tonight, the family that lives there came home to see—this.*

"This" is a remarkable picture of a van flipped sideways against the front wall of a house, its right front tire hugging the living room window. Any news director with experience in more than twelve markets would instantly recognize the gaper potential in this picture. It's the sort of image that any normal person would slow down to watch if they saw it on the highway. This makes it the gold standard of local news, the Fundamental Rule on wheels—the sort of thing you build lead stories around.

So, the story of the car crashing into the house is an obvious choice to lead the second half of "Live at Five," ahead of the breast implant story and even before the next weather report. The critical issue for the newsies is not whether to lead with this story, but how to structure the piece so the image of the crash appears as often as possible.

Riddle: How many times can one car smash into a house?

It would be possible to squeeze all the news value out of the car crash with 10 seconds of videotape shown over the anchor reading a brief account of what happened. It's easy to find 10 seconds of news here because, even though no one was injured in the crash, a van doesn't collide with someone's living room every day.

The difficulty comes in trying to embellish the incident to find a rationale for showing the crash pictures over and over. Let's look at the embellishments added to this story so it would time out at 1 minute and 40 seconds, and keep score of the number of times we see pictures of the crash damage.

We've already heard the words associated with Embellishment 1, as tape of the accident rolled over the banner headline "Big Mess" during Lisa's opening lines. There was a front view of the car sitting against the house, followed by a side view of the car sitting against the house. Score: 2 repetitions of the accident.

Lisa: *The chase started at a nearby school and ended when the driver ran out of control, right into the house.*

Lisa has already related the principal information about this story: what happened (a car smashed into a house), where it happened (in Carson), when it happened (tonight), how it happened (the driver ran out of control), why it happened (the car was in a high-speed chase with sheriff's deputies). An inexperienced news director might be tempted to leave the story here and go on to something with relevance to a greater number of people, such as a profile of celebrities who have fallen on hard times. But, a mistake like that would certainly make it unlikely that he would get that thirteen-week contract extension he'd been coveting. A veteran knows this is just the beginning of what matters in the story, not the end. She knows how to build a report around the pictures by sending a correspondent to the scene.

Lisa: *"Eyewitness News" reporter David Ono talked to a very stunned family tonight. He is live at the Carson sheriff's substation. David?*

David: *Lisa, you've got to feel for the family caught in the middle of this huge mess. It's a scene you'd never expect to come home to—a van smashed into the front of your house.*

This allows for Embellishment 2: The reporter's professional insights about our expectations (and David's news instincts are good—you never would expect to come home to a scene like this) supply cover for a close-up view of the car sitting against the house. Score: 3 repetitions.

Eyewitness: *The house looks pretty messed up.* (No additional pictures, but bonus points to the eyewitness who knew what to say to get on television.)

David: *It's the end result of a high-speed pursuit that started a few blocks away at Carson High School.*

Embellishment 3: As David again tells us that the crash was the result of a high-speed chase that began at a nearby school, we see footage of the van being yanked away from the house by a tow truck. Score: 4 repetitions.

Next up: a sound bite of a sergeant from the sheriff's department, who gives us details about the route the van was taking. This segment is of little use to anyone not actually featured in the story itself, with the possible exception of car/house crash groupies interested in retracing the route, although he does use words like "perpetrator" and "suspect." And, his words provide an opportunity for Embellishment 4: footage of people milling around the accident scene, followed by footage of people picking through the damaged van. Two more views of the accident. Score: 6 repetitions.

We leave these pictures to find David inside the house, ready to go with Embellishment 5: pictures of boarded windows and broken glass. *From the inside you can get a good look at the damage. As I pull away this curtain, you can see that this wall has been caved in about a foot to a foot and a half and this window was completely shattered.* Score: 7 repetitions.

It's time for the personal angle. David tells us the family that lives in the house doesn't speak English. So, they used another tongue to express their disbelief at what they saw when they arrived home. While David is telling us this, he shows us more of what they saw in Embellishment 6: pictures of more people milling about the van. Score: 8 repetitions.

We now need an eyewitness to tell us you never expect something like this to happen to your house, but it happened.

Eyewitness: *You never expect something like this to happen to your house, but it happened.*

While David demonstrates sound investigative skills, deducing who is likely to pay for the damage *(hopefully, their insurance company)*, we are presented with the opportunity for Embellishment 7: pictures of broken glass in the living room, pictures of a broken white picket fence outside. Score: 10 repetitions.

We now have the answer to our riddle. Without adding any new or useful information, this story was lengthened by a minute and a half by applying seven distinct embellishments that permitted footage of the crash to be repeated ten times. By sticking with the basic formula for generating news, very little creativity was needed to turn this piece into lead story material.

But, why stop here? There must be other great footage out there of car crashes where no one was seriously hurt.

5:31:40 PM: MINOR INJURIES, MAJOR PICTURES

We skip to a different city but experience the same idea.

Carol Cavazos: *A terrifying wake-up call for a South Phoenix family this morning. This is what Lorraine Chapman and her eighteen-month-old daughter woke up to. A car that had smashed into their bedroom,* *stopping only a few feet from her bed. Neither Chapman nor her daughter were hurt. The woman driving the car was treated for minor injuries.*

This version of car-meets-house included images of the car sticking through the outside of the house, a wooden beam resting atop the smashed car window, a view of the car from inside the house, and a picture of the mother and child walking into the house through the opening left by the car. Four images were shown in 15 seconds. Imagine what might have been possible if this had been the lead story.

Now take a look at this accident on Pinnacle Peak Road near I-17. Two people suffered minor injuries when this school bus from the Deer Valley School District collided with a truck carrying a steamroller and a load of tar. Fortunately, there were no kids on the bus.

Okay, maybe I'm stretching things, because no house was involved in this one. But, this story featured one aerial and three ground shots of the accident in just 15 seconds. Had these three events occurred in the same metropolitan area and appeared in the same newscast, our grand total for the vehicular damage section of "Live at Five" would have been eighteen images in 2 minutes and 10 seconds, an average of about one new accident perspective every 7 seconds. And the anchor could warn you to protect your house against this "unexpected rash of vehicles slamming into homes." It sounds so good that, if you were a news director, you might start to wish that you could make these stories up.

5:32:10 PM: WICKED WINDS

It's been 8 minutes since our last weather report, far too long by any reasonable standard. The forecast hasn't changed, so a creative approach is needed to make the weather feel like a different story. Let's see if you've become a veteran viewer. The creative approach appears below, in the form of a brief weather story. See if you can figure out which story you've already seen most resembles this one. I'll give you choices in a minute, and I'll help you along by underlining the key passage:

Lisa: *Well, wicked winds ripped through the Southland today, taking down trees and stirring up trouble. The strong gusts in Palmdale whipped up a tumbleweed twister* (**Video:** Tumbleweeds jumping high in the air and sweeping across a highway). *The dust devil swept clumps of dry brush across fields and roads. <u>While it didn't cause any damage, it made for a fantastic sight.</u>*

Dallas joins us now with the latest on today's forecast.

Okay, which of the following stories makes the same news assumption as this one? Is it:

    a. The nonriot?
    b. The dangerous restaurant?
    c. The "Hollywood Shootout"?
    d. The Great Baking Powder Incident?

If you said a, you should advance immediately to the 5:42 PM segment, "You Can Be a News Director," because you're starting to notice the hidden patterns of the news report. The link between the riot and the Wicked Winds is that neither one amounted to anything, but the station had pictures that amplified what was happening. The giveaway line, *while it didn't cause any damage, it made for a fantastic sight,* is just a recycled version of *it probably looked worse than it was.*

You can almost hear the news director say, this tumbleweed thing looks pretty cool. Let's write something about it.

The other three choices illustrate different types of news decisions that excluded using available footage to make something out of nothing. The "Hollywood Shootout" took fake footage to tell a real story, the Great Baking Powder Incident used no footage to tell a nonstory, and the dangerous restaurant used sordid murder details to retell an old story.

Each type of decision has its appropriate place, depending largely on the available videotape and on how long it's been since you last said something dramatic. This, in turn, is largely determined by whether it happens to be May, November, or February. You'll find out what I mean next, as "Live at Five" continues.

And you probably recognize that as a tease.

5:33:55 PM: TEASE

Ken: *Coming up: our "adults only" report on extreme sex.*

5:34:00 PM: AD TIME-OUT: MAY IS THE CRUELEST MONTH. FEBRUARY'S NOT SO GREAT, EITHER

Several times a year, the Nielsen people—those are the folks who like to ask us about our TV viewing habits—go in-depth (as the newsies might put it) to find out the truth behind the news shows we say we watch. They send diaries around to select people across the country to find out when their televisions are on and what they're tuned in to. The results are tabulated as ratings that measure audience size, which in turn determine how much the station can charge advertisers. The higher the rating, the larger the audience, the greater the price of commercial time.

These periods are special times for the talkers, the newsies, and everyone who makes his living on the air. They're called "sweep" periods, because of the way the Nielsen people "sweep up" the diaries in a fixed pattern that starts in the Northeast and works its way across the country to the West Coast. Small differences in ratings points can mean big differences in station revenues. Accordingly, they can also make big differences in the size of the market where everyone from the anchor to the news director will find their next job. Big ratings, and it's off to Nashville or Portland. Disappointing ratings, and it may be a one-way ticket to Bay City. Dismal ratings could land you in appliance sales.

So, every November, February, and May, TV people stock up on Rolaids and do their best to put out a product that maximizes the Fundamental Rule. This means rolling out the most gripping, the most exciting, the most entertaining news shows of the year. A crime that would merely "rock a normally peaceful neighborhood" in April would "leave residents reeling in disbelief" in May. A "potentially dangerous" January snowfall would "pack a punch perhaps potent enough to be the storm of the century" if it had the good fortune to strike in February. A warehouse fire is "dramatic" in October. In November, it's "dramatic *and* suspicious."

Understandably, this takes a lot of creativity and a lot of energy. The *Thesaurus of Clichés and Aphorisms* goes into overdrive (to borrow a phrase from the *Thesaurus of Clichés and Aphorisms*). Drama must be coaxed from every story, or created if it does not naturally exist.

The Sweeps Supplement to the Fundamental Rule says that in November, February, and May, explosive news is the only news. Stories with modest entertainment value that might appear in other months—like stories without celebrities or fires in them—are strictly forbidden by the Sweeps Supplement. Mayors and city councils might as well take these months off, unless they're celebrity mayors that do something dramatic, like set fire to the city council. Charitable organizations seeking media exposure had best disappear, too, unless they plan to be the ones to put out the fire.

You've probably seen statistics that say violent crime is declining in most major U.S. cities. These statistics do not take the Nielsen ratings into account. Nielsen statistics suggest that violent crime is declining in most major U.S. cities nine months of the year, with dramatic peaks in November, February, and May.

This turns November, February, and May into difficult months, both for the people producing the news and those of us watching it. The Sweeps Supplement assures that more *potential* problems *could* arise during these months than at any other time.

In November, February, and May, more buildings are engulfed in flames; small fires are "raging infernos."

In November, February, and May, there are more deadly intruders, more rampages, more hostage situations.

There is more dramatic footage of attacks that could have been deadly.

More security cameras capture disturbing pictures on tape.

In November, February, and May, teens who frequent shopping malls the rest of the year suddenly "maraud" in "packs."

In November, February, and May, more unsolved murder cases are inexplicably back in the headlines.

There are more bomb threats and ominous warnings. More simmering controversies erupt. There are more suspicious deaths, and more unidentified bodies appear.

More police cars are ambushed although, miraculously, no one is hurt.

In November, February, and May, there are more undercover sting operations, and you won't believe your eyes when you see what they turn up. More mechanics, repairmen, and sales agents are conspiring to rip you off. There are more cases of flesh-eating bacteria.

There is more controversy in November, February, and May than at any other time of the year.

It has even been reported that November is the most dangerous month to drive, a statistic gathered independent of Nielsen's influence, but which is a happy coincidence for newsies looking for every edge in applying the Sweeps Supplement. It means more chances to uncover remarkable highway video that, with a little luck, may become the most treasured kind of story in November, February, and May—"news you won't see anywhere else."

5:37:00 PM: SECOND FEATURE: EXTREME SEX

As Sylvia continues to cheat on her husband Kenny by sleeping with Danny and Reggie, and as Jake continues to cheat on his gay boyfriend Jeff with his overweight buddy Tiny, we are about to receive soothing confirmation that our friends from Sally and Ricki aren't as unusual as they may at first have appeared to be. "Live at Five" is about to go underground to reveal that a sexual playground regularly rocks suburbia, with the promise that the world of syndication is tepid compared to what's happening in the bedroom next door.

I, for one, sleep a little more comfortably knowing that skilled investigative reporters are carefully scrutinizing the bedroom next door.

It's the second Special Report of the evening, and anyone with a social conscience will want to see it. You probably suspect as much from the somber nature of the subject, but if you need a strong cue about the weightiness of the story, you can find it in the earnest way anchor Ken Matz looks at you as he says:

You may have heard about it, but perhaps you've never seen it. It's the hidden world of extreme sex. Tonight, "News Ten"'s Luann Cahn takes a revealing peak at some lifestyles where—(extended dramatic pause)—*almost anything goes.*

Hidden. Extreme. Almost anything goes. By now, we know it's not unusual for anchors to dress up a story. In this case, you get the feeling they're dressing it up just to undress it. It's a tease for a tease.

But any self-respecting local news organization would have to approach the story this way, because our expectations about what passes for healthy sexual behavior were set more than an hour ago by Sylvia, Reggie, and Tiny—not to mention Solo and Vixen—during their cathartic experiences with our syndicated humanitarian hosts. Teasing the tease is the least of our producer's worries.

A far more critical problem lies in the fact that the core premise of this story—that people are having sex—is not strong enough to satisfy the reporter's cardinal rule about how news should be, well, new. We all know that people have been having sex for a long time, at least since the Sixties. Many of our older cities are losing population, but they're not disappearing completely. So, it's hard to fathom the news judgments that go into deciding to run a story like this.

"However," you ask yourself in a fit of clear thinking, "what if the angle that justifies this story is that we're not just going to talk about dull, garden variety sex. Our audience is sophisticated enough to realize that if you talk about something way out of line, like *extreme* sex, you've got a great news story by anyone's definition!" If you've reached this conclusion, you're thinking like a news director.

Now, all you need to do is find something that makes Vixen and Solo look tame, and you've got a piece worthy of the Special Report designation.

But, that presents a different sort of problem than the conceptual difficulty you were wrestling with before. The locale for this story is Philadelphia, not Las Vegas or L.A. I would imagine that "extreme sex" is not the first thought that comes to mind when people imagine a trip to Philadelphia. "Honey, the automobile club's running a special Philadelphia getaway, featuring a private tour of the Liberty Bell and extreme sex."

No matter what the chamber of commerce may do, Philadelphia is unable to shake its image as not being an extreme sex kind of town. Neil Diamond can sell out the Spectrum in Philadelphia. Five nights in a row. You get my point.

That leaves the correspondent with the unenviable job of scouring the Philadelphia area for anything that can be billed as extreme sex. What she finds has to be conveyed in the proper ponderous tone established by Ken's introduction. And she needs pictures that will be shocking enough to be billed as extreme without violating the boundaries of good taste established earlier this afternoon by Jerry Springer.

Let's see how well she does:

In rapid succession, we see a clip of dancers in a music video—a pole dancer and a woman's naked back—as the word "sex" appears lots of times in letters of varying size in a constant crawl across the top and bottom of the screen. The image of a smiling, unidentified man crosses left to right, as if floating free from the confines of the physical world—a nice touch. As he traverses the screen, he says, *"Sex, sex, and more sex—it's the way to go, baby."* Luann concurs: *It's in our songs, it's on television, it's on the Internet. Sex: It's part of everyday life.*

Well, okay, I guess it is. It's certainly on the news. But so far, Luann hasn't said anything to clarify why it's on the news. You might even begin to think the story was little more than a ploy to show naked backs and shoulders. But, this is major market television; Luann knows what she's doing. Quickly, she gets to the point.

Let's talk about what's not so everyday for most of us. Strip clubs? Kindergarten, compared to the hidden world of extreme sex available in this town.

The chamber of commerce should look up and take notice.

A source, identified as a "former swinger" named Bob, runs down a list of available activities in the extreme underbelly of the City of Brotherly Love.

Bob: *Amateur video, swingers, strippers, nude dancing, lap dancing— you can get it all in Philadelphia.*

I'm sure Luann figures you're concentrating on the silhouetted image of a pole dancer while this quote goes by, and not thinking that the "kindergarten" strip clubs she dismisses as tame are the places where you'll find Bob's extreme world of strippers, nude dancing, and lap dancing.

So, Philadelphia has strip clubs. It would be news if it didn't. We have to do better than that, or at least show more pole dancers.

How about more from Bob, whom Luann tells us *is the publisher of several magazines that look like, well, they look like this.* I know, you're expecting images of extreme sex. But all you see are the printed words "hot" and "sex" on what appears to be a tabloid newspaper. *He and his wife say they experimented in the world of the extreme for eighteen years.* Okay, maybe a personal revelation from Bob will add a little credibility:

Bob: *As far as different sexual encounters for the evening, you know, if there's ten couples there, there's probably going to be four encounters or something.*

At this point, the news director is going to do the math. Ten couples, twenty people, four encounters. That leaves as many as twelve people, possibly more, without a claim to anything extreme. We have to do better. I can imagine him saying, "Get me something real extreme. Maybe a professional submissive."

I can imagine this because the story abruptly turns to highlight "Lisa," who is billed as a "professional submissive."

Professional sources always lend an aura of credibility to a story.

Luann: *This woman isn't into swapping. She's into spanking. She says people pay her $175 an hour to live a fantasy.*

"Lisa": *There's a lot of men that are into it. It's like the naughty little girl scenario.*

"Lisa" appears from the side, her dark hair brushed away from her bare shoulder and tastefully covering her face. Her name appears in quotes, so we can believe "Lisa" is just an exotic fabrication for her real name, which is probably something like Passion or Godiva.

We look over her shoulder to see Luann looking back at us in what professionals call a "two shot." Luann is seated but leaning forward toward us, her right hand placed thoughtfully beneath her chin. Her expression suggests she is treating the subject with the gravity it demands. In fact, she looks like she's about to ask an important policy question to a head of state.

Luann: *Who is your clientele? Who are they?*

"Lisa": *I have lawyers, accountants, doctors.*

And no wonder—at $175 an hour, these may be the only professionals who charge higher rates than "Lisa." I can imagine the news director again, saying, "Get me more extreme!" I imagine this because the next thing Luann says is:

You want more extreme? Try the world of Mistress Christiana. It looks like some bizarre set for a horror movie, but this dominatrix says it's her office. This so-called dungeon of bondage and discipline is in her suburban home.

In the suburbs—now *that's* a story. Herbert Finkel and millions like him could be unknowingly living next door to a dungeon of bondage and discipline. Set within this context, who knows what was really going on when Herbert heard his loud bang.

We're finally getting extreme. Except we're getting away from sex. Mistress Christiana says so:

Mistress Christiana: *It's a power thing; it is not a sex thing.*

Luann: *She claims this is her lifestyle and her career, but she also says she and her clients never have sex.*

Well, regardless of what Mistress Christiana thinks, the mental health expert we're about to hear from disagrees. And, after watching television for 1 hour and 40 minutes, we badly need a mental health expert. By permitting us into the dungeon, Luann has taken us so far into the world of the extreme that we might start feeling a little guilty that we're still watching. Cue the balding, middle-aged psychologist in jacket and tie, seated in front of the fake plant, to separate us from whatever secret pleasure we may be feeling.

Psychologist (sternly): *That's weird.*

I'm not a trained clinician, but I believe "that's weird" is professional, nonjudgmental diagnostic language for "that's sick."

Psychologist (even more sternly): *It's abnormal sex. The person that comes to them is getting some sort of a sexual charge, because of some abnormality in their make-up.*

Distanced from the patrons in the dungeon, we can feel relieved that we're not weird like they are, just normal, everyday voyeurs taking in serious journalism.

For her part, Luann has finally established the extreme credentials she so desperately needed, freeing her to close the piece with a serious statement of just how unusual this stuff is—spoken, of course, over more footage of exotic dancers.

Luann: *Psychologists tell us only about two percent of the population is into sex this extreme. Those who make a living in this underground sex world say most of their clients are married, seeking a fantasy they can't get at home.*

5:39:55 PM: WHAT'S REALLY IMPORTANT IN PHILADELPHIA

Ken: *Well, let's get right to the weather. It's what everybody's going to be talking about tomorrow.*

What did I tell you about Philadelphia?

5:40:00 PM: EXACTLY WHY DO THEY NEED WEATHER REPORTS IN SAN DIEGO?

Since we're back to the topic of weather, exactly why are weather reports needed in San Diego? Couldn't the San Diego television stations videotape their weather reports weeks, even months in advance?

"Looking ahead to the next five days, it should be sunny tomorrow with a high around 72 degrees at the beaches and 85 degrees inland. Tuesday will turn out sunny with a high around 72 at the beaches and 85 inland. Wednesday looks sunny, with a high of about 72 along the coast, but we could see readings near 85 inland. The outlook for Thursday is sunny with a high approaching 72 by the water, closer to 85 inland. It should be 72 and sunny on Friday, but look for the mercury to hit 85 inland.

"I'll be back later in the hour for a look ahead to the weekend."

I think even I could pull that off while pointing at the blue wall.

5:42:00 PM: AD TIME-OUT: YOU CAN BE A NEWS DIRECTOR

Maybe you're taking this all in and thinking, "I don't want to point at a blue wall. I'm not interested in being a weathercaster or a newswriter. Give me real power. I want to be the keeper of the Fundamental Rule."

If this idea appeals to you—and why wouldn't it?—then your place may well be as news director at a major metropolitan television station. The news director is, indeed, the symbolic keeper of the Fundamental Rule, the person responsible for turning the material components of a news operation—lights, wires, videotape, egos—into a show we can't turn off.

Not that being news director would give you *real* control over anything. Far from it. Perhaps you've seen those people who clean skyscraper windows, perched fifty stories in the air on a temporary platform attached to the outside of the building by a thin cable. That pretty much captures the situation of the typical news director. If you take away the cable.

You don't just walk into a job like this. Maybe you've worked for a while with one of the talkers like Jenny or Montel or Jerry, maybe you've even worked your way up to the point where you've produced one of their programs. You've seen syndicated television from the inside, and you know how to fashion the "Great Issues of Our Day" for the world of make-believe. You feel confident that you can apply your approach, your vision, to major market local news. You can show other newsies your record of success. You're ready to be a news director, and you're qualified.

You're qualified not only because of your resume, but because of your willingness to walk knowingly into a job that devours its young. To lawyers, accountants, and doctors, I would bet you could add television news directors as Mistress Christiana's most reliable customers. A dungeon of bondage and discipline would provide them with the perfect way to unwind after work.

The main outlet for a news director's creativity is his ability to set the tone for the newscast. But, this is also the main source of the pressure he may feel. Let's say you're hired by a station to fix a program that's hemorrhaging viewers. You look around, size up the situation, and realize that your anchor team won't talk to each other off the set. In other words, you have a chemistry problem. You fall back on your experience producing the talkers. You want to trust your first instinct: "If the anchors hate each other," you think to yourself, "let's let them punch each other out on the set during the newscast. We can even have the sports guy play the bouncer."

Soon, you're relieved to have kept this instinct to yourself, when you recognize that your anchor team consists of a pregnant woman and a former pro wrestler. You realize that such a match-up would only play well with males under eighteen, a demographic that typically does not watch much local news.

So, you go to work brainstorming about ideas that have worked in other markets, trying to figure out what you can do to change things at your new home. Rather than fighting, you think, you can introduce more laughter. Break the tension with humor. Everyone responds to laughter. And, as we have repeatedly seen, the news is filled with funny moments.

Now, it's time to implement your policy, to create the illusion that your anchor team is chummy by having them joke easily with each other. If they're good at what they do, the anchors will have no difficulty convincing viewers that they're best friends, that they probably hang out with each other after the show.

Your job now is to make sure the laughter doesn't get out of hand. You'll need to issue policy directives to your anchors. More than five deaths in a story should be treated tactfully, with poststory banter limited to mild blather with minimal giggling. Never laugh during or after a story that contains the phrase "mass graves." Otherwise, apply normal, common sense standards of decency and respect.

How well it works will be measured by what happens to your audience. You will have a grace period to turn things around, possibly as much as a week. At which point you will be confronted with the latest ratings for your program, and the station's general manager will evaluate your audience size and composition. If things are moving up, your job is safe for another week. But, what if you face trouble?

Here's an example of something that could go wrong. To see if you're cut out to be a news director, see how you would handle it.

You're called in to the general manager's office six days after implementing your approach to news. He assures you that you're on the right track, even likes the new slogan: "Party On with NewsTeam Seventeen." But, it seems there's a small problem. Your audience share has slipped below two. In statistical terms, less than two percent of the television sets that are tuned to anything are tuned to you. Put another way, more people are watching reruns of Gilligan's Island at eleven. And they're watching in black and white, no less.

And to compound things, the wrestler's Q Score is down. That means he's less appealing in this new format than he used to be. Apparently people don't find a laughing wrestler to be credible.

You need an answer, and you need one now. If you're up to the job, you realize that asking for more time won't work. You've already been given six days. What's your approach?

Although there's no single solution that's bound to work, if your response contains any of the following elements, you're ready for prime time.

First: Claim success. Point out that since you took over, the audience has been walking away in smaller numbers than before. This should be an easy case to make. With ratings as low as yours, there were very few people left to walk away.

Second: Argue for a new set. Everyone likes a new set. A new set is fun, and sensible. You can get it done without having to answer to the anchors. And it takes time to assemble, thereby stretching out the time you'll need to update your resume.

Third: Update your resume. In your updated resume, claim success. And be sure to emphasize that you were the driving force behind the new set.

5:45:00 PM: SCORE!

Now..."Big Board Sports." KYW News/3 continues.

Todd joins us with the sports tonight, and Todd is a lifelong Clippers fan. How is that team doing?

Only in a sports report will we find out such personal information as Todd is a lifelong Clippers fan. Marc or Robin probably have political affiliations, but you'll never hear one introduce the other by saying, "Marc joins us now with a story on President Clinton's job performance, and Marc voted for President Clinton twice. Marc, how's the president doing?"

Sportscasters can be different because sports reports are different. Sportscasters have to be partisans. When the sports report is on, the whole news crew becomes one great example of the Local Angle.

"Well, Robin, I'm pleased to see that the president's job approval rating is up four points to fifty-eight percent."

You'll never hear that. It could offend up to forty-two percent of the viewership. But, no one has a different opinion about local teams, or if they do, they keep it to themselves.

You know, a lot of Clipper fans are starting to say they're my Clippers again, because, what the heck, they're playing some pretty hot basketball lately.

Sportscasters can get away with saying things like this just as easily as they can get away with using expressions like "what the heck." Imagine an anchor saying that. "A lot of people are saying Bill Clinton is my president again, because, what the heck, he's presiding over a pretty hot economy."

Sportscasters are just different. They have names like Dickey and Skip. Anchors have names like Guy.

The Local Angle gives sportscasters a free pass to say just about anything they want. If two politicians are known to hate each other, Guy will never tell you about it in so many words. But Skip will.

The Red Wings and Coyotes do share one similar trait: hate. They hate each other equally. How much hate? This much. (Two players crash into the hockey rink glass.) *How about some of this?* (One player chokes another with his stick.) *Or a little bit of that?* (One player punches another.) *They had to call the security guards.*

I'm getting Jerry Springer flashbacks.

Of course, you might say that if one politician hates another, he nonetheless would be unlikely to express this by choking his rival with a stick. You can be pretty confident that no matter how nasty things get, George W. Bush will not try to choke Steve Forbes.

On the other hand, hockey players are paid to act out even when they don't have any feelings about their opponents. So, two politicians could really dislike each other, and it will never be reported, whereas sportscasters can make a big deal about an athlete's so-called hatred of an opponent even though it's all just an act. That makes coverage of it perfect for television. It conforms to the Fundamental Rule.

Skip may not even know how players on the Red Wings and Coyotes feel about each other. But, no one is going to ask him to reveal his sources.

No one will question his judgment as long as he shows action footage, uses great adjectives, and covers the Local Angle.

First period Wings are wild—and it's four to one Detroit. But the doggies bite back. Relentless—they cut it to four to two.

If he can pull off a line like "the doggies bite back" with a straight face he's worth every cent he's paid.

5:47:55 PM: NOW, AN AD FOR AN AD

Larry: *After fifteen years in the biz, Dave Letterman has reinvented late night TV. Coming up, I'll take you behind the scenes of his hit show.*

5:48:30 PM: THIRD FEATURE: IMPLANTS

It's been 42 minutes since Lisa McRee first raised the tantalizing prospect of sharing scary stories about breast implants, and we've waited patiently through three weather reports to hear the actual news. This would seem to be a pretty good time to end the waiting.

The problem is, the first tease contained all the actual news in the story: *Scary stories about breast implants haven't stopped the rush to get them.* Since then, additional teases for this story have allowed our local anchors to invoke Fundamental Rule Postulate 26 three additional times, enough to make any viewer feel he had earned the right to find out the scary details.

But there are no scary details, at least not tonight. And this poses a dilemma for any good news director. We already know how to handle stories that contain no news. But what do you do when you have a story that's devoid of the action footage, frightened neighbors, and fearful circumstances that make news reports so interesting?

Normally, this would be a ridiculous question to raise, because any news director with a prayer of keeping his job for more than the thirteen-week industry average would shoot down stories of this sort before they had the chance to contaminate "Live at Five." But the implant story is an exception because it's a Backwards Story.

Most stories work in a forward direction. They are hyped throughout the newscast by a series of teases that build up to the main event. The teases exist to boost the story. In a Backwards Story, the teases are the main event. In the case at hand, the teases provided our station with the cover it needed to repeat the term "breast implants" in the apparent performance of a public service, when in reality nothing interesting about breast implants awaited at the end of the trail.

In the case of a Backwards Story, it's tempting just to air the teases without the story and hope the audience forgets they were promised a segment. But that might appear unethical or, more importantly, it might undermine the station's credibility. When viewers notice inconsistencies like this, they tend to blame the anchors. They write letters to the station. It can get ugly.

So, it's best to treat the dilemma directly. If we can't produce a viable story that lives up to the expectations set by the teases, at least we can make it seem like the segment is more than a weak excuse to copy one of Ricki's favorite topics.

Let's see what we have to work with. Laura Diaz has filed a story about two women who went to Costa Rica to get implant surgery they could no longer acquire in the United States. They think it's safe. So does their overseas doctor. A couple of U.S. doctors have their doubts about the advisability of surgery abroad, but they feel pretty good about the implants themselves, which they contend pose few risks. That's it.

Having a woman file this segment is an important touch, because a male correspondent could make it appear as if the station were exploiting the subject, especially if he gave the impression that he was enjoying the story too much. So, chalk up one point for the news director.

Having a good action quote also helps make the story seem like a story. Here's one from an implant recipient attesting to how happy she was with the medical experience she had abroad: *For what it would have cost me to have my implants here, my husband and I went to Costa Rica for twelve days, and with food, airfare, hotel, and my surgery it ended up being, like $200 cheaper.* If you weren't listening too closely, you could easily think this was a promotion for a luxury cruise—food, airfare, hotel, and surgery included, taxes and transfers additional.

The best way around the dilemma of what to report is obvious if you return to the basics and remember why this Backwards Story exists in the first place: Postulate 26. If the teases offer an ideal opportunity to mention breast implants, the story itself provides opportunities for numerous variations on the phrase. Let's see how well this story did:

"Breasts" are mentioned five times.

"Implants" are mentioned twelve times.

"Enlarged" and other references to size are mentioned three times.

Not bad for 2.5 minutes.

Pictures, of course, really communicate the point of any story, and there's no reason why a Backwards Story should be different. Perhaps the most illustrative pictures in this piece reenact the consultation between doctor and implant recipient prior to the operation. Discreet and professional, they evoke the nobility of the medical profession and the sanctity of the doctor-patient relationship. You're looking over the shoulder of a shirtless woman, directly at a doctor in a white medical gown. The doctor, gesturing with his hands in front of his chest, says, *I want you to tell me what idea you have about the size.* Cut to a frontal view of the patient, made possible by the strategic placement of long hair.

It's as if Postulate 26 has come to life.

5:50:50 PM: AFTER THE SURGERY

Guy: *Is your stress level putting a crimp in your love life? Coming up, we'll show you what you can do to keep stress from ruining romance.*

5:51:00 PM: AD TIME-OUT: YOU CAN BE A STAR

Many people have at one time or another fantasized about sitting in the center chair of a news set, staring down the red light on the camera that indicates your image and words are about to travel live to an entire metropolitan area. I don't think it's such an unusual wish, when you consider how many of our shared experiences are made possible by television. Like the heralds of an earlier time, the anchor is at the vanguard of everything important in our collective consciousness, sort of a town crier in make-up. More than the people behind the scenes, even more than the revered weathercaster, the anchor holds the star spot in the electronic galaxy.

It is a tantalizing prospect to imagine yourself in that star spot, with the anchor desk all to yourself. It's about far more than just being on television. We've already agreed that that's going to happen, considering the need for all those neighbors and eyewitnesses. We've already reviewed what you need to say when your moment comes, and I'm sure with some practice you'll be ready. No, this is much bigger than simply having 4 seconds of fame. This is about the full 15 minutes. It's about facing up to and conquering the quintessential self-doubt of our day: You know you've got what it takes to be Herbert Finkel. Do you have what it takes to be Guy?

Sadly, most people do not. It takes a special kind of person to be an anchor, and it's not just about having great hair. In fact, probably one of the biggest misunderstandings about television anchors is that they're all show and no business. There's an unfortunate stereotype about television anchors that has to do with their ability to put a Q-tip in one ear and pull it out the other. If that were true, far more people would be qualified to join their ranks.

Although it is certainly the case that some anchors—and out of respect, we should call them "the talent"—are unwilling or unable to distinguish nouns and verbs without painstaking assistance, it is also quite typical for them to devote those long hours between on-air appearances to developing their news copy. Visit a newsroom before airtime, and see how commonplace it is for the talent to be secluded in a quiet corner, drawing inflection and emphasis marks on that evening's copy. People who automatically think "airhead" when they hear the term "anchor" miss the point: The talent is the program's one indispensable component, the place where all the planning and sweat, all the hopes and aspirations of an entire news crew come together. The talent brings life to fantasy. He is the front end of the Fundamental Rule.

Unless his Q Score tumbles during sweep month. Then, he's packing his bags for Duluth faster than you can say "back to you, Lisa."

Do you have what it takes to succeed in an arena where so many before you have failed? Unlike newswriters and weathercasters and news directors, there are many intangibles involved in making a star. But, there are at least two things you can look for, because every successful anchor has them. They will not guarantee that you'll one day be sitting behind a lovely wood-grain Formica desk making breezy conversation with Dickey or Skip. But without cultivating these two things, your quest for the top spot is likely to end in futility.

The first one is trust. The second one is caring. Trust is in your face. Caring is in your voice.

You're going to be the one telling people to be a bit more careful tonight because a menacing mongoose, one of a rare species of carnivorous ferrets, has escaped from the metro zoo. You don't want people to panic. Worse, you don't want them to run to the encyclopedia, where they might learn that the greatest danger posed by this slinky mammal is to poisonous snakes. You need to strike the right balance between concern (epitomized by the word "menacing") and reassurance (which comes from your inner knowledge that no one is really at risk). You do this by communicating trust.

Trust is in your eyes. It's in your ability to make eye contact through the camera with thousands of people you cannot see. Trust is in the way you look.

I would be less than honest with you if I said that anyone can look the part. It helps a lot to have a symmetrical face, and unfortunately not many people outside the modeling ranks really do. People are simply more likely to trust someone with a symmetrical face. By symmetrical, I don't mean something most of us have, like one eye on either side of the nose. I mean having each eye set precisely the same, pleasing distance from the nose. Too close and you can look shifty, too far and you can look dull-witted. Neither of these encourages trust.

The nose should be neither too big nor too small for the face. Hair should be full and either very blonde or very dark. Men can be gray, but should never be bald unless they want to do sports or weather. Women should never be bald under any circumstances.

We could go feature by feature like this, constructing a face that communicates trust, a face that people will respond to. Look closely at a picture of Bill Clinton. His major features really don't go together—the bulbous nose, crinkled eyes, big chin, and the like. But his face works because his features are remarkably symmetrical, communicating trust even when his words raised doubts. It's no wonder he was elected in 1992, against George Bush (lips too thin—should never have told people to read them) and Ross Perot (ears too big—probably shaved ten percentage points off his vote).

Before you give your anchoring prospects another thought, you'd be best to grab a tape measure and calculate the sizes of and distances among your key facial features. Millimeters matter, so be sure to measure carefully.

If your face doesn't balance, you may need to take steps to smooth your way to the anchor desk. Some relief can be provided with make-up, lighting, and camera angles, although you shouldn't consider yourself a failure if you find yourself thinking of permanent cosmetic surgery. It's a big investment, and there may be some risk and discomfort involved. And afterward you still may not achieve your goal, but it may open up career avenues you never anticipated, like politics or selling upscale used cars.

If you're on the cautious side, you may want to work on caring before you invest heavily in trust. Caring is in your inflections and cannot be developed through expensive corrective surgical techniques.

Caring is much harder than trust. Many people, even the most sensitive among us, never get the hang of caring. Many people *feel things* for others, of course, but that has nothing to do with broadcast caring, where feelings are of little use to anyone if they are poorly expressed.

Caring on television means being able to communicate caring, regardless of how you may feel.

In particular, a successful anchor needs a repertoire of caring. She needs to identify the appropriate emotion in a story and communicate that she feels it. She needs to assume the relevant cheerleading role in her banter with the sports reporter. She needs to affect the appropriate degree of lightheartedness as she presents dessert. And she needs to treat the weather with the deep, abiding respect it deserves.

It's easy to see how many ways the talent can trip up. An anchor with perfect pitch could nevertheless draw on the wrong feeling, smiling devilishly through that sweep-month story on flesh-eating bacteria when a more appropriate choice would be studied concern tempered by revulsion. He could inadvertently separate himself from the city's last-place football team, maintaining a sense of ironic distance in his introduction of Skip, when the time-tested pose of communal self-deprecation would be far more effective. He could laugh too hard at the weather report or make too many jokes about the meteorologist's bad toupee. Even a symmetrical face would not save him here.

This is why being the talent is such a demanding job, and why those who do it well are rewarded with high salaries and countless invitations to civic lunches. There's really no formula in place to create a successful anchor the way you can create a successful newswriter or weathercaster. To those of you who still wish to try, I wish you good luck. But, I'd advise you first to try something a bit more modest. Find a car dealership, spend a week on the lot, and see how well you do. If you can convince people that you have a once-in-a-lifetime low price on a rare, preowned vehicle, but it expires the second they leave the showroom, there may be a place for you in the big time.

Trust me.

5:55:30 PM: MORE SEX, PLEASE

The on-screen graphic is distressing and portentous. It says, "Too Stressed for Sex," and although it doesn't appear to apply to Jerry or

Jenny's guests, or to the folks going abroad for implants, or certainly to any members of the extreme sexual underworld in Philadelphia, it may at this point apply to you. After all, you've been watching these people for two hours.

Maybe Guy can help put things back in perspective.

Guy: *Stress in a relationship can ruin your sex life, but there are some ways to avoid it and keep the romance alive.*

We need unnamed experts.

Guy: *According to the experts, getting out of the house to exercise is a great way to relieve stress in your love life.*

We see a couple sitting on a couch watching television. Remember, getting out of the house to exercise should never take precedence over watching your favorite network program.

Guy: *Set aside some special time away from children and other distractions. Other options include talking and listening to each other, to be supportive. And never criticize each other during romantic moments. No surprises, but it'll take a little work.*

Especially during November, February, and May.

5:56:00 PM: DAVE LOVES CHEESESTEAKS

One of the most important characteristics of the ratings sweeps is news programs are not the only ones being evaluated. During this intense and important time, the entire network is under the microscope. The price the network will be able to extract from advertisers at all time slots hangs in the balance, and everyone at the network feels the stress. It's a time when network executives need to be especially attentive to getting out of the house to exercise.

When something as important as advertising is at stake, networks become happy families. They pull together. There's a Network Ancillary to the Sweeps Supplement to the Fundamental Rule that says, during sweep periods, news shows will be the friendly cousins of entertainment shows, working together toward a common goal. Fortunately, the Fundamental Rule ensures the kinship will be an easy one, because news and entertainment shows are, after all, genetically related.

Under the circumstances, news programs can be forgiven for indulging in what under less important conditions might be seen as blatant self-promotion for the network. You're about to see one of these instances. It's a news story about an entertainment show. If you were unaware of the special pressures of the ratings sweeps, you might think it was simply a long, self-serving advertisement during valuable news time.

Larry: *We're sure a lot of you are going to watch the Dave Letterman anniversary special tonight on CBS and here on Channel Three. Surviving fifteen years on late-night network TV is no small feat. In fact, Johnny Carson is the only late-night host to last longer.*

By now, we're sophisticated enough to reach below surface impressions. Think of what's coming as more than hawking the network's late-night fare in an attempt to build an audience. Think of it as a hard-hitting investigation. In fact, think of it as a "Special Report."

Larry: *In this "News Three" Special Report, I will take you behind the scenes for a closer look at what separates Dave from the rest of the pack.*

The graphic over Larry's shoulder reinforces his words. It's a picture of Letterman in front of the logo for his program. Above it are the words "Special Report." We're about to go behind the scenes. We're going to take a closer look. We're going to find out what separates Dave from the rest of the pack.

So, it's only reasonable that this investigation should begin with the opening sequence to Letterman's show, followed by a montage of scenes from his prime-time special. Larry explains why his report is so newsworthy:

Dave is marking his fifteenth anniversary in late-night television with a month-long celebration.

Larry is on a first-name basis with Dave. Like any good journalist, he demonstrates an intimate knowledge of his subject.

For his part, Letterman has a less noble perspective of what's going on.

Letterman: *It's just kind of a cheap way to call attention to ourselves.*

Count on Dave to be irreverent.

Larry: *Dave laughed, ridiculed, and clowned his way through more than 2,500 shows on NBC and CBS. Altogether, he's had on 8,594 guests on his show. But not all are Hollywood celebrities.* (We see pictures of Hollywood celebrities.) *Letterman has showcased an array of the weird and the unnatural.* (We see pictures of the weird and the unnatural.) *Through it all, Dave says he's lucky to have the kind of career everybody dreams of.*

We see Dave on the "CBS Evening News" set, waving to the camera as Dan Rather delivers the news. It's a nice way of reminding us of Dave's news value.

It doesn't take long for Larry to find the Local Angle in his Special Report.

Larry: *During a recent satellite interview, I asked Dave the question that's on everyone's mind here in the greater Philadelphia region.*

You might expect that the question on everyone's mind is "What is Mistress Christiana's address?" considering how extreme sex has taken hold of the Philadelphia suburbs. But, Larry's mind is somewhere else.

Larry (to Dave): *Dave, the big question right now in this town is, when are you gonna to do your program from Philadelphia? I mean, this is the birthplace of it all, you know?*

Dave (to Larry): *It's getting to be a little embarrassing that we haven't been to Philadelphia. But, I think the next time we do one of these four city deals, or whatever it turns out to be, we gotta go to Philadelphia. There's just no reason not to.*

You can only imagine how hard it was for Dave to give Larry a straight answer, considering the available collection of time-tested Philadelphia jokes. But, Dave is invested in the Network Ancillary, too. Perhaps it's that kind of professionalism that Larry had in mind when he promised to show us what separates Dave from the rest of the pack.

Larry: *After my in-person interview with Dave last year, he hounded me for an official KYW jacket like our camera people wear. So, we decided to spend a few bucks and send him one.*

To the uninitiated viewer, this may seem like an odd transition that takes us away from the central purpose of this Special Report. But, think about what Larry is doing. By making reference to a *second* interview with Dave—and an *in-person* interview at that—he's bolstering his credentials as a correspondent. Larry knows Dave. Dave asks Larry for gifts. In fact, Dave hounds Larry. Their relationship goes way back, at least to last year. Unconsciously, we're reassured that Larry is the best person at KYW to file this report. It establishes Larry's credibility as a journalist, which, in the news business, is everything.

Dave (to Larry): *I want to tell you something, Larry. You people have gone nuts down there in Philadelphia. You oughta shut down your little TV operation and go right into the sports clothing industry.*

We see a still picture of Letterman on his set, wearing a KYW jacket. The picture fades to Larry, again sharing the screen with the "Special Report" logo. Larry smiles.

Larry: *You know, he hounded me for months about getting that jacket which costs a lot of money and, of course, I had to squeeze it out of the news director. We finally got it to Dave. He's so happy about it.*

The report is about to wind down, as is "Live at Five." If we're not dead by six o'clock, at least we're exhausted from what we've been through. We've gone behind the scenes. We've had our closer look. And we're ready to move on. Just one more thing:

Larry: *If you just can't get enough of Dave, you can catch a new "Late Show" after our late local news. Tonight, Dave welcomes Bill Cosby and Tina Turner.*

5:59:00 PM: LOCK THOSE DOORS—AND COME BACK AT ELEVEN

Later tonight on "News Three," heartache, uncertainty, and waiting— family and friends hoping for word of a missing SEPTA driver who vanished without a trace. A Norristown deacon faces shocking sex charges. And—can you believe it? There's a new product that's supposed to help you lose weight just by sniffing it. We'll test those claims tonight at eleven.

Later tonight, new developments in the incredible cops and robbers shootout in North Hollywood. New at eleven, did any of the brazen bandits get away?

And I'm News Hawk Joe Ducey. Later tonight, we set up hidden cameras and put local furnace repair people to the test. Would they overcharge? What can you do about it? Wait 'til you see what we found. A News Hawk investigation, coming up at eleven, on Seven.

I'm Michelle Muro. Tonight at eleven, we put your fruits and vegetables to the test. It's off to the lab to see what you really get with some produce. And, for the first time, surgeons have successfully reattached a person's tongue. We'll show you how they did it.

That's "Action News" for this evening. "World News Tonight" with Peter Jennings is next.

"Eyewitness News" continues at eleven. Now, "The CBS Evening News" with Dan Rather.

Up next, "NBC Nightly News" with Tom Brokaw. We'll see you at eleven. Thanks for looking in.

Hour Three: Network

6:00:00 PM: TEASE

Disembodied Female Voice: *The dictionary defines passions as extreme emotions or desires, uncontrollable anger, love, hate, intense romantic desire. And, this summer, all of the above. NBC redefines daytime drama with "Passions."*

Disembodied Male Voice: *NBC/10 and MSNBC. Get connected.*

Serious, staccato background music.

Disembodied Male Voice: *From NBC News World headquarters in New York, this is "NBC Nightly News" with Tom Brokaw.*

Tom: *The Pope cancels a Mass on a trip home to Poland. He's sick with the flu. More questions about his health. "In Depth" tonight: stolen cars, one every 23 seconds. Where they go, why it's hard to stop the crooks, how to keep your car out of their hands.*

Disembodied Male Voice: *From ABC News World headquarters in New York, this is "World News Tonight" with Peter Jennings.*

Peter: *On "World News Tonight"—the media madness in New Hampshire. Is it George Bush the candidate, or is it the media's herd instinct?*

Disembodied Male Voice: *This is "The CBS Evening News" with Dan Rather reporting from New York.*

Dan: *A gun-control battle of biblical proportions: The House votes to allow posting the Ten Commandments in schools to promote morality.*

And—hold the phone. An industry study raises new questions about the possible health risk of cell phones.

Lots of maps of the world float by.

6:00:25 PM: WAR STORIES

We'll begin our report tonight with war stories. Not the sort of heartbreaking reports from places like Kosovo and Bosnia that periodically dominate the opening segments of national news programs, but the stories that double for these when nothing of an urgent nature is happening in a country that at least thirty percent of Americans can recognize.

Just like the talkers and the local newsies, the network news folk thrive on conflict. With all the conflict in the world at their fingertips, you might imagine they have an endless supply of great stories. Just think of all the things that inherently involve conflict. Politics involves conflict. Making legislation involves conflict. And these are the sorts of things national newsies have always covered. You might think that all they need to do is keep on covering politics and policymaking, and viewers will keep on coming back. Their jobs should be easy.

But it's not that simple. Much of what happens in politics and policymaking involves conflict, it's true. But it's the wrong kind of conflict. It involves things like speeches and votes, things that are too slow or take more than 4 seconds to say. Usually, there aren't even any good pictures. Too many people tune out, and no wonder. After 2 hours of terrifying turbulence and transsexual prostitutes cheating on female impersonators, who wants to listen to the House of Representatives vote on gun control?

It's the wrong kind of conflict.

Wild teens out of control—now that's the right kind of conflict. Are big-breasted women blessed or cursed? Best friend betrayals. Freaky, roof-busting great balls of hail. We can make that work.

Will Congress raise the minimum wage? Now, we have problems.

Political stories involve boring conflict, which is the worst kind of conflict because it makes a joke of the Fundamental Rule. These stories *should* be a natural for television, because of all the beating up on each other political people do. But they're hard to convert into riveting news stories because they take too long to set up, well over the 2-minute maximum imposed by broadcasters. In the time it would take for a reporter to explain the rationale for the different positions people take on the minimum wage, you could be well on your way to switching to Turner Movie Classics. There might even be a great 4-second sound bite at the end of the story, something where a politician is really beating up on another politician. What good does that do if you're not around to hear it?

Compounding the problem is a long tradition that says the national newsies *have to* cover things like politics and policymaking. Overlooking things like national elections and major congressional debates could make a network news operation seem almost as if it were not serious about reporting the news, possibly bringing into doubt the credibility of your trusted anchor. Then, Dan and Peter and Tom might start worrying about whether people still believe them, about whether they're still Emmy material. Nobody wants that.

So, national newsies are saddled with the obligation to cover stories filled with boring conflict. It is a serious problem, which lends itself to only one solution. These stories have to be transformed into the right kind of conflict by skilled television professionals, people trained in the ability to pretend.

Political and policy stories may violate the Fundamental Rule, but people who understand television know how to use the Fundamental Rule to turn political and policy stories into good television. It just takes a little imagination. Here's how it's done.

Start with a type of story that the national newsies are obligated to cover but, unlike politics and policy stories, invokes easily understood references, moving sound bites, heated situations, and gripping visuals. War is a great example. It's hard to turn away from the torment and horror of war footage, even when a favorite episode of "The Dick Van Dyke Show" is playing on "Nick at Nite."

War is the right kind of conflict.

Now, imagine that the people who are running for president or voting on free trade really aren't running for president or voting on free trade. Imagine that they're at war. Suddenly, you're speaking a language that's instantly recognizable and irresistible to hear. Presidential candidates don't *simply* want to be elected. They're engaged in a death battle where their political lives are at stake—a battle all but one will lose! Senators aren't deciding whether to enact a complex trade bill. They're caught between hungry lobbyists and angry voters—they have to vote, but whom will they alienate? If they make the wrong decision, they *could* find themselves involved in a cutthroat election, engaged in a death battle where their political lives are at stake!

Now, you've got a news story. Now, you can take four really good seconds out of a campaign speech without having to go into the details of what the candidate is talking about. You can explain an intricate House debate without delving into the dull legislative details. That's the beauty of turning politics into war. You don't have to explain anything, except for the fact that politicians are out there fighting for their survival. Then what they're saying is no longer about what they're saying—it's about how they're saying stuff so they can survive. So, they can say anything, and you can cover it easily, the way it should be covered, with the right kind of conflict.

And it gets better. The war motif makes it easy to find the right kind of conflict in political stories on a regular basis. That's because once you see politics as war, you have a formula you can easily apply to any political situation. If you feel like you're back to where you were 45 minutes ago when you learned how to be a newswriter, you're putting it all together. The neighbors are gone, and politicians have replaced lone gunmen as the perpetrators of tragic incidents that eyewitnesses are calling nothing short of gruesome. But these are just alterations in the details, which we learned long ago are incidental to good television. The important thing is that you have discovered the right kind of conflict in stories you are obligated to do, and you can write these stories over and over again without succumbing to burdensome boring details.

War stories make great lead stories, and they lead the news tonight.

Dan: *Good evening. A rapid-fire switch on Capital Hill today in legislation to reduce youth violence. The make-or-break House debate on even limited measures to keep guns out of schools suddenly turned into a vote to put copies of the Ten Commandments in the schools. We go to CBS News chief Washington correspondent Bob Schieffer on Capitol Hill. Bob, what's going on there?*

Let's look closely at what just happened. Dan prepared us for a war story about gun-control legislation by saying congressional debate was "make or break." He didn't say for whom or for what. He didn't have to. Clearly, it's "make or break" for the legislators. That's the only reason they would engage in a "rapid-fire switch" on something—a nice bit of military imagery which, though still a bit vague, preps us well for the assault that's coming.

Then Dan invited Bob to tell us "what's going on there." When he did this, he pretty much wrote a blank check for his chief Washington correspondent. Bob could tell us about the details of the gun-control legislation the House is considering. He could instruct us on the way that legislation has changed as it worked its way through the long process of congressional decisionmaking. He could explain why some lawmakers see a relationship between teaching values and reducing violence, and the honest dispute they have with other lawmakers who believe youth violence can only be curbed by reducing the availability of weapons. I can see you reaching for the remote. So can Bob.

Fortunately, he can also disregard those details and tell us about the life-or-death struggle facing politicians forced to vote on a measure popular with constituents but unpopular with a powerful interest group—a struggle so ferocious that politicians will change the subject, stall, and do anything just to avoid making that choice. It's as if the politicians see themselves engaged in a death battle where their political lives are at stake. That's a story about war. It's interesting, and it works. So, Bob applies the formula, and tells us what's really happening.

Bob: *Well, Dan, this really isn't about the Ten Commandments at all. It's about gun control and background checks at gun shows. Members of the House of Representatives know that they're eventually going to have to vote on those fairly mild gun-control measures passed by the Senate. But with the gun lobby breathing down their neck hard now, they've been putting it off by talking about a lot of other things for as long as they possibly could. During debate on reducing school violence, they've managed to consider everything but tightening the gun laws, and this was the latest idea.*

Every army has its commanders, and every commander has a game plan for victory. The army in this story is the Republican majority in Congress. The objective in the larger war is re-election for all its members. This particular battle is about surviving an ambush by gun-control forces seeking to capitalize on a wave of public outrage against school violence by getting Congress to approve gun-control legislation.

Bob is telling us about the game plan employed by the congressional Republicans. They know they have to vote on gun-control legislation sent to them by the Senate, and it presents a serious dilemma in their fight to win the larger war. If they support the legislation, they stand to alienate the National Rifle Association, an organization that gives a lot of campaign money to a lot of congressional Republicans. If they oppose the legislation, they stand to alienate large members of the public who at this moment are urging Congress to do something about youth violence. To survive the upcoming election, they need both money and votes, so they can't afford to alienate either group. Their "latest idea": Change the subject. Say the way to curb school violence is to make schools post the Ten Commandments. That's a popular position with voters, too, and it doesn't place limits on gun sales. The public will think they're acting responsibly while they avoid a nasty gun-control vote, which will make the National Rifle Association happy. It's a great ploy.

Of course, putting it this way makes it sound as if congressional Republicans were only pushing the proposal as a matter of convenience—you know, all's fair in war and all that. It's just a tactic in a delay strategy. It makes it sound as though they really didn't care about whether the Ten Commandments were posted in classrooms or, for that matter, whether school violence diminished. Certainly that's what their opponents thought.

Bob: *Opponents saw it as yet another tactic to delay the vote on guns.*

Perhaps they're right, and perhaps they aren't. The beauty of covering the story this way is it doesn't matter, because tactics don't have to be principled—they're just tactics.

The only remotely interesting reason to consider the merits of the Ten Commandments proposal is if somewhere in the debate over the issue, someone said something that made a great sound bite. Like this:

Bob: *Besides, opponents asked, which Commandments?*

Rep. Jerold Nadler: *Which version? The Catholic version, the Protestant version, or the Jewish version? They're different you know.*

That's worth a 4-second detour in the story.

Bob: *Members brushed that off as detail.*

Detail doesn't play well in war stories. But another good 4-second sound bite would.

Rep Mark Souder (holding two large blue tablets representing the Ten Commandments): *I hope I don't drop these. I don't want to bring any bolts of lightning on us.*

This would be an excellent time to bring in Charlton Heston, the National Rifle Association president who in real life got to play

Moses in the movies. But that might have gotten in the way of the wrap-up to the war story, the part where Bob tells us how the debate he's been talking about for 90 seconds is meaningless, except to permit congressional Republicans a tactical midnight retreat.

Bob: *For all of the rhetoric, there is virtually no chance that the Commandments will ever be posted in schools. There's very little support for this in the Senate, no support for it in the White House, and in the past the U.S. Supreme Court has ruled such action unconstitutional. But in the meantime, and clearly by design, the votes that really count on those gun laws probably won't come now until late tonight when most Americans are sleeping. Dan?*

6:02:10 PM: EXCUSE ME?

The nice thing about all this is that politicians really do engage in strategic maneuvering, just as Bob said. Of course, they're not engaged in a real war, but Bob doesn't have to make up any of the details to give us an accurate account of the tactics they employ. He just has to put aside any pretense that lawmakers are interested in things tangential to getting re-elected, like making laws. This makes war stories far more substantive than news about riots that never happened or wicked winds that caused no trouble. No one is going to look at the situation in Congress and say, "It probably looked worse than it was."

All this is fine, provided the combatants in war stories act like the generals they're supposed to emulate. But there are times when this does not occur, times when politicians inexplicably fail to follow the script provided them by the networks, times when they even appear to be motivated by principle. Without doubt, these moments are rare. But when they happen, reporters need to be very creative.

Here's a good example, from the archives. As the 1996 presidential election was winding down, Bob Dole was being advised by his campaign generals to attack Bill Clinton's character in an effort to get reporters to stop talking about how Dole was hopelessly trailing in opinion polls. They wanted to keep reporters from saying stuff like,

84

Dole's aides privately fear that if Dole continues to trail badly in the polls, reporters will start questioning whether he is gamely campaigning in what he knows is a hopeless cause.

Candidates generally don't like stories where the word "hopeless" is affixed to their efforts and would generally regard a statement like this as bad press. But reporters will say this sort of thing whenever they feel they're covering a lopsided battle. Unless the losing side attacks, all reporters are able to talk about is how they are losing because they won't attack. They have no choice. There's nothing else they can do without departing from the formula.

In Dole's case, there was much consternation among reporters because he and his running mate Jack Kemp seemed *deliberately* unwilling to attack the opposing side. To reporters, it looked like they were either inept or badly misinformed about the life struggle they were in. It was as if they were purposely taunting reporters with civility, and reporters took note. ABC's John Cochran:

John: *Dole campaign aides grumbled that Kemp passed up every opportunity at last night's debate to attack President Clinton's ethics.*

Kemp: *It is beneath Bob Dole to go after anyone personally.*

John: *Before the debate, campaign aides say, Kemp had practiced zingers attacking the president for broken promises, Travelgate, and White House use of FBI files on Republicans. The zingers were never used. Today, Kemp said he did not need to highlight White House scandals.*

Kemp: *It wouldn't be Jack Kemp to bring up what the American people already know. My purpose is not to tear them down, but to build up our agenda.*

That's a noble gesture, but reporters would risk losing their license to practice if they didn't ask, "What is his deal? Doesn't he realize there's a war going on?" It would certainly make the reporter feel a bit better if he could find a sign that cooler heads recognized the importance of what was happening.

John: *Although Dole said Kemp did a great job last night, he acted like he had heard enough from his running mate. While Kemp spoke to a rally, Dole paid no attention, turning his back and posing for pictures with supporters.*

That's a little more like it. Maybe John read a bit into Dole's actions here—after all, he could have just had his back turned to Kemp because he wasn't interested in hearing his running mate's standard speech for the umpeenth time. It doesn't really matter. What's important is that John found in Dole's actions a creative way to illustrate how the top guy hadn't forgotten that a battle was raging.

Things got more difficult for John a few days later, though, when Dole himself refused to attack. Understandably, this left John at a point of desperation. It's one thing for a running mate to take the high road. But the standard bearer? It was almost enough to make Kemp look sincere when he said Bob Dole would not engage in character attacks—an impossible position to defend in the midst of battle.

This meant John had to be creative. He had no choice but to do the attacking for Dole. I don't mean to suggest that he became a partisan soldier in the Dole army. That would be unethical. But if Dole would not point out Clinton's flaws, at least John could talk about the flaws Dole refused to address in a story about how Dole refused to address them.

John: *Did Bob Dole attack Bill Clinton in harsh terms today? Yes, he did, plenty. But did Dole get personal, dig into the president's past, stir up the mud of Whitewater and other issues of character? No, he didn't.*

So, John mentioned it instead.

John: *Dole in person is still taking the high road, hitting the president hard on his record, but not going after Clinton on his personal life and moral behavior.*

Bummer.

John: *Some in Dole's camp wish that he would get nastier at this point, with the polls delivering constant bad news to the campaign.*

This is important to reinforce, because otherwise it might appear that John himself was on the attack. In John's report, you can almost see Dole's attachés trying to shake the candidate out of his slumber. You can practically hear them telling the candidate what John has been telling us. "Wake up, Bob," they might say. "You have to attack if you want to survive. The election's in less than a month. The winner gets to live in the White House. The loser is going to have to do television ads about erectile disfunction. And Bill Clinton isn't a credible spokesman for erectile disfunction."

Of course, we all knew how this one was going to play out. John knew it, too. There was little he could do but acknowledge how Dole's amiability had made him a boring and irrelevant failure. In a positive way, of course:

John: *Dole himself continues to be the gentleman on the stump. That may make for a duller campaign than some would like and perhaps a losing one. But it lets the candidate play out this possibly climactic moment in his career more like a statesman and less like a nasty politician.*

As this is a war story, the term "statesman" should be understood in the classical sense, meaning a politician without Viagra. Not someone you want engaged in a death battle where their political lives are at stake.

The cumulative effect of all this kindness can really take its toll on the network newsies. It's one thing to write a story that says Dole has retreated from the fight of his life. It's quite another to have to write that story every night for ten months. Understandably, the frustration this causes reporters can result in their doing something dramatic to protect their duty to use the war formula during national elections.

When reporters get tired of simply saying a candidate has failed to attack, they may find themselves resorting to extreme measures, like blaming the audience for demanding exciting television.

Jeff Greenfield: *We say we want more documentaries and high-class dramas on television. We watch sitcoms and "Melrose Place." We say* *we want healthier food. We chow down burgers and fries. And we say we want high-minded, civil, issue-oriented public debate.*

I know. It's a bit disingenuous. But it's a great way to lament how boring things are.

Clinton: *I respect Senator Dole and his record of public service.*

Jeff: *Last Sunday's presidential debate was a model of civility.*

Dole: *Thank you Mr. President for those kind words.*

Jeff: *And Wednesday's vice-presidential debate was even more polite.*

Kemp: *My friend Al Gore.*

Jeff: *When the debate ended, everyone commented about how "thoughtful" and "substantive" it was. Those are two well-known code words for "boring."*

This is a valuable and instructive point, and not just because it helps us decode the expressions commentators use. It also tells us everything we would ever need to know about the central role of the Fundamental Rule in political discourse. Jeff is saying that we're the ones who claim we want to be informed, when in fact we don't want being informed to get in the way of having fun. In turn, television news folks are obligated by the Fundamental Rule to give us what we want.

Jeff will now illustrate this premise with the use of some really gripping footage, just as soon as he dispatches with the dull set-up.

Jeff: *Despite those critics who called the Kemp-Gore face-off a tea party, some civility is clearly essential to a useful public debate.*

That was the dull set-up. But it's followed immediately by pictures of a huge chair-throwing melee on a 1988 "Geraldo Rivera Show." That's good reporting.

Jeff: *For instance, this is clearly entertaining television, but not civil.* Next, we see pictures of five dark-suited members of the Taiwan legislature having a fistfight. *This is certainly attention-getting legislative debate, but not civil.* Now the punchline. We see President Clinton giving a speech at a podium with five cabinet members sitting beside him. Former Secretary of State Warren Christopher is one of them. A close-up reveals he is sleeping. *This on the other hand is clearly civil discourse, but lacks a certain zip.*

Fortunately, good network reporters know how to find zip, even in an election that features Bob Dole. This assures us that even in the most trying of times, when national candidates act with civility, our republic will not be at a loss for amusement.

6:05:00 PM: BUT ENOUGH ABOUT YOU

Sometimes politicians will play by the rules and employ the tactics of warfare, and reporters nonetheless will forego reporting about them so they can cover what's happening to other reporters. This probably sounds odd to anyone unfamiliar with how network news reporting works. It may even seem a little inappropriate, maybe a bit incestuous for journalists assigned to cover politicians to instead cover one another. Nothing could be further from the truth.

There's a Self-Interest Addendum to the Fundamental Rule that obligates national reporters to cover what's happening in their own lives before they cover anything else. Only if there is no entertainment value in personal experience are they to turn to the lives of the people they're assigned to follow.

So, when a reporter goes to cover, say, a candidate, and finds a large crowd of other reporters, she's trained to think, "Wow, there are a lot of other people here just like me. There's news in that."

Perhaps you're thinking that there really isn't any news in a large crowd of reporters covering a politician. Politicians attract large crowds of reporters all the time. When they do, it's for a reason that's important in its own right. If reporters are covering the other reporters in the crowd, aren't they missing the point?

If you are thinking this way, you could benefit from a deeper appreciation of the Self-Interest Addendum.

Let's say you're sent to New Hampshire to report about George W. Bush on his first day of campaigning for the New Hampshire primary. The primary is still eight months away, which in political time is the equivalent of about seven years, because political time is calculated like dog years. This means there really is no battle to speak of, even though the candidate is doing his best to engage in tactical maneuvering for long-term advantage. But you showed up. You look around and see a lot of other people with notebooks and cameras, a lot of other people like yourself. They showed up, too. You think that's pretty interesting. The Self-Interest Addendum obligates you to look no further for your story.

Peter will provide the necessary introduction.

Peter: *In New Hampshire today, George W. Bush, who may not get all this attention several weeks from now, was attracting an enormous crowd of reporters and camera people for his first day of campaigning for the New Hampshire presidential primary, which is probably next February. There's a lot of pent-up interest in the Bush campaign, and, as ABC's Dean Reynolds reports, it is some crowd he's attracting.*

It's obvious to Peter—as it would be to any seasoned reporter—that the crowd of reporters is the real story here. Every news organization with a budget large enough to cover a rental car has sent reporters to New Hampshire to follow the Texas governor around as he meets with drain commissioners and attends pancake breakfasts. We need to know why.

Dean: *It is truly remarkable. George W. Bush is turning into a political phenomenon for reasons almost no one can explain.*

Translation: This is genuinely puzzling. Even I don't know why I'm here. I don't like pancakes.

Dean: *Here is the governor of Texas, who acknowledges talking about issues in only the broadest of terms with no specifics. But a huge press corps is hanging on his every word, and no one seems to know why.*

Translation: None of the other reporters I've talked to know why they're here, either. The governor is speaking in platitudes, and we're eating it up. It doesn't make any sense. Yet, here we are. And there are so many of us. This must be a story of historic proportions.

Dean shows us a lot of pictures to underscore his point. We see lots of cameras and those boom mikes with the long arms. There are plenty of people milling around, some carrying note pads, others with cameras around their necks. Bush moves tentatively through the crowd, and he is enveloped by reporters who seem to be pulled by the momentum of other reporters toward the candidate. The scene has a kind of other-worldly quality to it, a sense of aimlessness tempered by historic portent, sort of like Woodstock for journalists. Maybe the point is that, years from now, if there's a thirtieth anniversary of this event, Dean will be able to tell his grandkids that he was at the original.

To add credibility to his coverage, Dean needs a source. Typically, in a political story, the source would be a politician, perhaps even Bush himself. But the Self-Interest Addendum precludes reporters from even thinking about doing this. The only viable source for a story about reporters is another reporter. Since it would be bad form for Dean to interview himself about his attendance at "Bushstock," he simply needs to find a colleague who is willing to appear on camera.

David Kennerley: *You'd expect to see this at the end of a presidential campaign, not at the beginning.*

Dean: *David Kennerley is one of thirty-five photographers assigned to Bush, who made the covers of two out of three national news magazines this week.*

David: *This is the biggest scoop I've ever seen in thirty years of political coverage on somebody's inaugural voyage.*

We still don't know why this is happening, but we're certain now that something remarkable is going on with those reporters.

Dean: *You'll have to trust me but—that is the governor back there. I can't see him. Most of the voters here can't see him, because he's sur-rounded by the press. There are at least ten TV stations here from Texas* *alone and journalists from all over the world. As many as forty cameras are recording everything down to the boots he wore in Iowa or the street shoes he changed to in New Hampshire.*

We still don't know why this is happening, but we now know the extent of the phenomenon. And we've been able to look at more pictures of cameras and microphones.

Dean: *Bush did have a press conference today.*

But there is no point talking about it because, *he made little news and no mistakes.*

Then again, isn't that the whole point of "Bushstock"?

Dean: *And that may be the truth about why Bush's Republican opponents and reporters, even reporters covering reporters, are watching him so closely. To see who he is, why he is so popular, and whether he will stumble.*

So, who is he? Why is he so popular? Will he stumble? We will have to wait for another day to find out, for we have learned all that we are to learn from Dean. His job was to cover the groupies, a job he did admirably. As for the candidate, he seems curiously to miss the point of his own event.

Bush: *I like to talk about me, and I'm glad others are talking about me.*

Perhaps as the war moves on, they will. But that will have to wait for another day, too.

6:07:20 PM: UP NEXT

Dan: *Still to come on tonight's "CBS Evening News": Texans run for cover from roof-busting great balls of hail, in tonight's "Weatherwatch." And, an American dream turns in to a homeowner's nightmare.*

6:07:30 PM: PROMO

Deep Disembodied Male Voice: *"Dateline" tonight: It was almost the perfect crime—a senator's daughter murdered. The prime suspect: her husband, a bishop's son.*

Female Reporter: *How vicious was this murder?*

Male Source: *As vicious as they get.*

Disembodied Voice: *Two powerful families at war. Will it all end in the electric chair? A "Dateline/Court TV" exclusive.*

On the next "Extra!": Think you're alone? Think again. Hidden cameras stole this woman's privacy. Now, see how someone could be watching you. Next on "Extra!"

Only on CNBC: "In Profile" with Bob Costas. Now, in revealing personal stories, the people you read and hear about come to life. "In Profile," on CNBC.

6:07:45 PM: AD TIME-OUT: LET'S HAVE AN IMPEACHMENT!

I have a feeling that had Dean watched that last promo—the one for the "In Profile" series on CNBC—he might have found an important clue to the question he never answered, about why "Bushstock" was such a tremendous draw. While the network is taking 2 minutes to pay its bills, let's look at this riddle more closely.

It went by quickly, but I think the promo said something about "revealing personal stories" where the people you "read and hear about come to life." I think that captures the early appeal of George W. Bush. Dean admitted that the governor wasn't really saying anything important, and that people really didn't know him. But lots of people knew *about* him, recognized his name. He was famous. Lots of people were giving him money: He was wealthy. They were giving him money to run for president: He was powerful. He was on television a lot. That alone could explain his popularity.

When you're famous, wealthy, powerful, and, most importantly, on television, you can have a hundred press conferences where you say nothing, and no one will care that nothing was said, because what matters most is that you showed up. When you have a place in the media constellation, the fact that you exist matters more than who you are or what you believe. You are a star in an industry that demands stars. You are a star by virtue of your fame, a star because you are famous. Reporters will flock to your events without knowing why, as if they were hypnotized. And, in a sense, they were hypnotized by the glow of celebrity that shines forth from you and warms all in attendance, making reporters newsworthy celebrities by association.

It's no wonder Dean found news in the fact that he was there.

In our system, politicians function most effectively when they recognize they are popular culture figures. They only get in trouble when they want to do things like debate legislation and pass laws, things that have no real place on television.

Bob Dole didn't realize this until after he was soundly defeated, something that might not have happened if he had recognized the power of sharing the stage with David Letterman while the campaign was still going on. After the campaign, people started to comment on how relaxed Dole seemed as he joked with late-night talk-show hosts. It was as if he felt that he could indulge in a little celebrity banter now that the serious business of running for president was behind him, never recognizing that indulging in celebrity banter is what running for president is all about.

Bill Clinton knows this instinctively, which is why he has survived as an icon almost as long as Madonna has. Ever mindful of his reputation, it's why he engaged in the publicity stunts that led to his impeachment. Ever mindful of his legacy, he knew he would be remembered for weeks, possibly months, as the central figure in the greatest pop-culture orgy since the O.J. Simpson trial—indeed, as the greatest pop-culture figure of the past three years. The Monica connection became public at a time when we were so starved for a shared experience that yesterday's figures, has-beens like Joey Buttafuoco, were experiencing a resurgence. The newsies and the talkers were at a loss for how to capture the public's imagination. Even Tonya Harding was waiting in the wings. Things were becoming intolerable.

I can imagine what a meeting of network biggies would have been like a couple of years back, when the pressure was enormous to fill the celebrity gap. "Wouldn't it be great," one executive producer might have said, "if we could have an impeachment!"

"Wow!" a senior producer would exclaim. "Let's do it!"

"The biggest TV star in the world on trial for his political life," a younger producer would echo. "That would be awesome!"

They could cast it easily, with Bill as the slick but vulnerable protagonist and Kenneth as the smart, determined, but slightly demented prosecutor. They would choose Judge Judy to officiate, except for the constitutional provision that gives that job to the Chief Justice. Lots of power would be at stake. The lines between good and evil would be slightly smudged. It could run for months!

All they would need was a crime. And then it happened.

Bill Clinton saved us from a pop-culture recession that was threatening to be as severe as any since the invention of pop culture immediately following World War II. And he did it on a scale consistent with what we have come to expect from him. The saturation coverage that would become the most prominent feature of the Lewinsky era rivaled everything that came before it. Entire cable networks got a new lease on life. Even Geraldo Rivera experienced a comeback.

Never in the long history of television news did a story get as much saturation coverage as Monica did during that heady first week when the story broke. According to one count, the three major broadcast networks together aired 124 Monica-related items—more stories than they aired for every other Clinton scandal combined. Seventy percent of the news that week was about Monica. The Pope was arriving in

Cuba for a visit billed by the networks as historic—so historic, in fact, that they sent their trusted anchors to Havana to cover it. Then came Monica, and most units were pulled back to Washington and New York. It was an understandable change of plans. Monica Lewinsky is a more important figure than the Pope, who has never made a surprise guest appearance on "Saturday Night Live."

It was to be the nation's first pop-culture impeachment, the hallmark of which would be that, like everything else on television, it would have no staying power. No question, it produced lots of pictures— Monica getting out of a limousine, Monica sneaking into a building, Monica getting into another limousine. It was the obsession of the moment. But there was also this vague feeling that we had somehow seen it all before, and several hours after it ended, it was hard for many people to remember that it had happened. Perhaps a song will come on the radio from time to time that will send you back to the Monica era, briefly reminding you of where you were and how you felt when the House voted on the four articles of impeachment. But that will be it.

That's what makes the Clinton impeachment so different from the only other one in U.S. history, the 1868 impeachment of Andrew Johnson. People are actually still talking about it 130 years later. Johnson was the president who assumed the office after Lincoln was assassinated. He was a southerner who didn't see eye to eye with northerners in Congress on how to reconstruct the South after the Civil War. Johnson's impeachment raised questions about who was a U.S. citizen, about how the nation should be reunited following its most tragic and divisive war to date, about how the emancipation of slaves should be conducted.

Clinton's impeachment turned on questions of what did the president touch, and when did he touch it.

But as weighty as it was, Johnson's impeachment simply didn't have the panache of the Clinton affair. No one, to my knowledge, referred to the House managers who prosecuted Johnson as *a conservative dream team*, the way their Monica–era counterparts were described on NBC. Although I haven't looked through all the historical records, it's doubtful that anyone wondered whether Johnson appeared sufficiently contrite in the statement he made following his Senate acquittal.

However, since the TV show "Politically Incorrect" did not premiere until the 1990s, I am confident that there was no counterpart to the appearance on that program of Democratic Sen. Robert Torricelli and Republican Rep. Joe Scarborough, who, according to MSNBC, *joined Joan Rivers for a gossipy, vulgar discussion of the Lewinsky scandal.* I'm certain that Civil War–era Sen. Edmund G. Ross and Rep. James M. Ashley never chatted it up with Joan while making tasteless jokes about their different views on the Emancipation Proclamation.

I am equally sure that no one ever gave Johnson makeover tips, the way Monica was inundated with advice on how she should look and sound. But Johnson didn't have the counsel of MSNBC:

Note to Monica: Before you go out on the talk-show circuit—or look for another job—you might want to do something about that "Valley Girl" voice. Here are a few makeover tips from the experts.

"I'm a little let down by what I hear," said voice trainer Jeffrey Jacobi. "If I were an employer, would I want to take the time to set aside a meeting with this woman? I would be less likely to."

Neither was there any nineteenth-century counterpart to "Team Monica," the personal entourage that followed Lewinsky everywhere she went and attracted a lot of coverage as a symbol of what it takes to survive as a cultural icon.

Wherever Monica Lewinsky goes, she is supported by security, publicists, attorneys, and advisers. When someone calls her hotel room, it's a publicist, not Lewinsky, who answers the phone. Whether Lewinksy likes it or not, she is going to be living in a fishbowl, and she will have someone looking over her shoulder all the time. It's the kind of attention few people want or have ever experienced.

Lewinsky's first postscandal public appearance could help shape the future of Monica, Inc. How she looks, how she is dressed, how she handles herself—her facial expressions and body language—are all very important.

That should go without saying. On television, they are the most important things of all.

6:10:00 PM: AL GORE GETS A SURPRISE MAKEOVER

That's why politicians are rarely content with their media images, why they are restless to reintroduce themselves to the American people, sometimes trotting out two or three versions of themselves in the same year to see which one works best. Like engineering student Ruth who got a surprise makeover from one of our favorite talkers, they're simply brushing and touching up what was there before to see if they can look better on camera.

Of course, because this type of behavior cuts to the heart of what it means to be a political leader, newsies are invariably there to cover it—sometimes even going in depth.

Tom: *NBC News "In Depth" tonight: It's Al's turn. With more than a year to go before the nominating conventions and two days after the GOP's leading contender, George W. Bush, announced he's running, Vice President Al Gore announced his candidacy. Today, the focus was on a new message. Beginning our "In Depth" coverage tonight, NBC's Claire Shipman.*

Claire: *He's one of the most recognized men in America, but he believes even after almost twenty-five years in public life, voters still don't really know him.*

It's a little hard to fathom what it means to be on television for twenty-five years and be unknown, when the definition of being known is being on television. But that is the burden of the Gore campaign.

Claire's reporting promises to take us behind the scenes of the Gore announcement, and explains how the candidate intends to address this burden through the careful selection of sound bites.

Claire: *Perhaps the most critical part of Gore's message: They may be partners, but Al Gore is not Bill Clinton.*

Gore: *I felt that what the president did, particularly as a father, I felt that it was inexcusable.*

Claire: *New, tougher words about the president and the Lewinsky scandal, intended to create distance. It's all part of the Al Gore makeover.*

Monica, take note.

Now, doing a political makeover is very tricky. In addition to great sound bites, the candidate needs to select from a list of possible images and find several that he thinks will play well on the air. Not every image will fit every candidate. Similarly, not every image is appropriate. Sandy can get away with shoveling earthworms out of a box of dirt to proclaim her love for Rodney, but that probably wouldn't work for Al. He needs to be more like Jenny or Ricki or perhaps Sally, someone Sandy could confide in later. Only not too much, because there isn't enough time to hear every voter's life story. It's a delicate balance.

Deciphering the work the candidate is doing to find the right image takes great care. That's probably why Claire had to go "in depth" to file this report.

Watch what she does: By detailing the images Gore has selected for himself, she gives us insight into the process by which celebrity is created.

Claire: *Gore needs to create a new image for a candidate widely described as boring.*

Claire is right to make Gore's boring problem the first item in her report. Nothing is more devastating to a politician than to be perceived as boring. Boring is not entertaining. You can get away with a lot of things in politics—you can even be dull-witted—but you cannot be dull. If he cannot address this, he cannot survive.

Fortunately, this is just a makeover, not a real change of any sort. Gore really can be boring, as long as he figures out a way to appear interesting on camera. This gives him hope. Claire captures this nuance as she itemizes the different images the vice president will attempt to assume.

Claire: *Image number one: moral leader, surrounded by family, devoted to his wife of twenty-nine years—an implicit contrast to Clinton.*

We see Al, Tipper, and kids waving and smiling, behind the headline, "Moral Leader."

Claire (to Gore): *Are you worried that you will pay the ultimate price for Bill Clinton's impeachment?*

Gore: *We are two different people.*

Claire: *But not when it comes to Clinton's successes. Image number two: engineer of the nation's prosperity and man of substance, with plans for everything from education to the environment, in contrast with Republican George W. Bush and Democrat Bill Bradley.*

Under a picture of Gore at a podium, the on-screen headline "Engineer of the Nation's Prosperity" fades into the headline, "Man of Substance." This sounds credible: You must be a man of substance if you have plans for everything from education to the environment. So far, so good. But the hardest is yet to come.

Claire: *Image number three: Al Gore, not just a wooden politician, perhaps the most difficult to achieve.*

The on-screen headline says, "Not Just a Politician." Perhaps out of respect to Gore's office, the word "wooden" is omitted.

In a long sound bite, Gore searches for ways to demonstrate his humanity.

Gore: *I'm a Vietnam veteran. Uh, I went to divinity school. Uh, I had your job as a reporter for seven years.*

Claire: *On day one of his campaign, the race is clearly on to redefine the image of Al Gore. Claire Shipman, Iowa City, Iowa.*

Inexperienced viewers might question why the network devotes attention to the process of how the candidate decides what to say instead of covering the things the candidate actually says. These folks might actually expect to see coverage of what's in Gore's plans for everything from education to the environment. But skilled viewers realize that the actual plans have nothing to do with becoming president because they are not exciting. Gore might even get into trouble with some voters if they knew what he planned to do, trouble that could make him unpopular. Didn't Dean just tell us that George W. doesn't have any plans? And he's a phenomenon.

Years from now, Ronald Reagan's economic and foreign policies will be a distant memory, but people will remember him as the guy with the airport in Washington, D.C. It can take a lifetime of great sound bites to achieve that level of immortality. When network news covers imagemaking while it is happening, they show us history unfolding. If Al Gore should one day become an airport, you will be able to say you were there when it all began.

6:12:00 PM: DOWN TO SIZE

The prospect of becoming an airport must be unusually enticing to Bill, Al, and George W.—the people who aspire to high office. Because no matter what they do right, they must inevitably submit themselves to media scrutiny of what they do wrong. Reporters are obligated to reveal the dark side of being famous, just as they are obligated to cover themselves whenever a lot of them show up to a big event. It's in the handbook, just like how to cover a crime scene.

The process is simple, and it works like this: People who are stars because they are famous are obligated to do something entertaining to maintain their favored position on television. The thing they do must contain the right kind of conflict. If you're the president, you're therefore obligated to have phone sex with a young intern, or at least bug the national headquarters of the opposing party. If you don't, reporters will have to find something wrong with you, your politics, your ambition, or your past. It's not their fault; it's simply procedure.

That's why it wasn't unexpected when Tom followed the cheery story about Al's surprise makeover with a piece that raised serious concerns about the last five people who held the office that Al and George W. covet. Things were becoming too upbeat, and we needed to return to reality. So, as Al figured out a way to become a Man of Substance and Engineer of the Nation's Prosperity, at the same time...

Tom: *At the same time, there's a new book out today on the American presidency and what's happened to it since Watergate. The author is Bob Woodward, the Watergate reporter who went on to fame and to become one of Washington's most astute students of the people who have power and how they use it. The book is called* Shadow. *It's a cautionary tale of what's happened to the Oval Office and those who occupy it.*

A blow-up of Bob's book appears over Tom's right shoulder. Behind it, the last five presidents, walking solemnly astride their wives, appear in succession. It is our cue that this is going to be a serious and important story.

But we should already be aware of the magnitude of this story, because Tom told us that Bob is a famous author, someone who *went on to fame* as a result of his Watergate reporting. Bob is a celebrity, just like Tom and the presidents in his book. That is why the publication of his new book requires 2 minutes of national news attention. If Bob wasn't famous, his observations wouldn't be credible, and there would be nothing to this story besides a blatant advertisement for his book. By the same logic, when Tom does stories about *The Greatest Generation* or Peter features stories about *The Century,* they would just be tastelessly promoting their best sellers—if they weren't famous.

Fortunately, Tom and Peter are very famous, which makes them experts on which famous people to feature in stories about other famous people. For something as big as a new Bob Woodward book, a big production is in order: a full-screen graphic of a waving U.S. flag; a montage of the last five presidents taking the oath of office; and an interview with Bob, of course, conducted by none other than Tom.

Tom (to Bob): *When Gerald Ford took office after the resignation of Richard Nixon, he went to the American public and uttered that memorable line...*

Ford: *Our long national nightmare is over.*

Tom (to Bob): *Do you think it is?*

Bob doesn't need to consult the manual about how to respond so that you get on television. Bob lives on television.

Bob: *It's not. That's the problem.*

Tom (to Bob): *Five presidents—Gerald Ford, Jimmy Carter, Ronald Reagan, George Bush, Bill Clinton. Common themes there?*

We see a full-color close-up of the book.

Bob: *One of the common themes is they all have their famous denials.*

Here comes the dark side.

Tom: *Beginning with Ford and the Nixon pardon.*

An image of Ford in grainy black-and-white and tilted slightly to the right appears on the screen. It looks pretty ominous.

Ford: *There was no understanding, no deal.*

Bob: *It turns out, at least, that one was offered.*

Now it's Carter's turn to appear grainy and tilted.

Carter: *I will never lie to you.*

Bob: *He fudged and cut and told half-truths way too often.*

Reagan (grainy and tilted): *We did not—repeat, did not—trade weapons or anything else for hostages.*

Bob: *And then, having to say, oh yes, I did.*

Bush: *There was no quid pro quo.*

As Bush speaks, the camera zooms in on his grainy black-and-white image. It's the scariest picture of all.

Bob: *And then confiding to his diary, I'm one of the few people who knew all of the details. And Clinton, in the most famous denial of all:*

Clinton: *I did not have sexual relations with that woman.*

Bob and Tom are telling us about the ordeal of being president. One day you're running for office, and you're a political phenomenon or moral leader. Then you win and become a grainy, off-centered, scary black-and-white guy.

Fortunately for Bob, his celebrity isn't dependent on holding elected office. Not that this would disqualify him from having his flaws exposed in a public forum should the appropriate occasion arise. It's just that an interview with Tom isn't that occasion. Tom identifies with Bob. A little background:

Tom: *Twenty-five years ago, Watergate. Woodward and Carl Bernstein were becoming famous as the reporters who broke the story.*

A full-screen picture of Bob's earlier book, *All the President's Men,* floats toward us.

Tom: *I was covering Nixon for NBC News.*

Pictures of a young, dark-haired Bob Woodward working at a typewriter fade into pictures of a young, dark-haired Tom, microphone in hand, standing in front of the White House.

Tom: *It was one of the biggest stories of our time.*

Maybe this piece isn't about the presidency after all.

Tom: *In his book, Woodward characteristically has some fascinating details of backstage conversations, about the Persian Gulf War, about the Nixon pardon, and about Iran-Contra.*

If Bob wasn't famous, that might seem like a blatant plug for his book.

Tom: *I'll have more of my interview with Bob Woodward tonight on "Dateline," at eight Eastern.*

And if Tom wasn't famous, that might seem like a blatant plug for his evening show.

6:13:35 PM: TEASE

Tom: *I'll be right back with some new information on "The Fleecing of America," how our money is still being wasted.*

6:13:40 PM: PROMO

The Cher exclusive. Cher kicks off her world tour, and only "Entertainment Tonight" can take you backstage. The wigs. The costumes. We're inside Cher's dressing room and behind the scenes. All the last minute madness as Cher takes the concert stage for the first time in eight years, later tonight on "E.T."

"Can You Believe It?" Only on KYW/3 "Eyewitness News," tonight at eleven.

6:14:00 PM: AD TIME-OUT: FEAR AT 6:16, OUTRAGE AT 6:20

We're entering the "Fear and Outrage" portion of the newscast. I thought you should be warned.

The purpose of the "Fear and Outrage" portion is the same as the purpose of everything that's come before it: to make sure you stay tuned in for the weather segment that lies ahead at 6:26 PM. But fear and outrage are different and distinct. You will get the most out of the upcoming stories if you recognize how professionals regard each.

Fear is regarded as: "a feeling of alarm or disquiet caused by the expectation of danger, pain, disaster, or the like; terror; dread; apprehension."

Outrage is thought to be: "any act grossly offensive to decency, morality, or good taste."

There's a long-standing debate among network newsies about the best feeling to generate from a story, fear or outrage. Some at the networks—and I believe this is a minority position—advocate fear. They believe fear is the most primal human response, the sort of thing that, in the extreme, will immobilize viewers to the point where they won't be able to lift the remote control. Most of these people have worked in local news.

Majority opinion lies with outrage. Unlike fear, outrage appeals to our minds. We have to think about something to be outraged about it. It requires a certain amount of sophistication. Unlike fear, outrage makes us want to act. Outrage advocates are interested in getting viewers to the point where they want to break the remote control. Most of these people started their careers in politics.

Because the desired effect is the same in either case, the debate may seem like an empty one, like arguing whether skydiving is a greater thrill than bungee jumping. Not for network newspeople. The fear versus outrage argument can be an intense one, especially during November, February, and May.

Because neither side has been able to win a clear victory, most network news programs contain a mixture of fear and outrage stories. Each type of story is the product of knowledgeable experts employing a carefully honed approach to the news. But each approach is distinct, despite the similar effects of the stories.

We'll look at two examples of each approach, beginning with fear and concluding with outrage. Pay close attention. During the next commercial break, you'll have a chance to take the "Fear and Outrage Challenge," where you can try your best to correctly classify a real network news story.

6:16:00 PM: SCARY CARS

The key to writing a good fear story requires finding something to be afraid of. That may sound obvious, but in practice it often takes a good deal of creativity. Back in the days of the Cold War, events themselves produced great fear material that needed little embellishment from network reporters and producers. There's nothing like the credible threat of total annihilation to keep viewers engaged.

Today, it's not so easy. You can't rely on viewers to automatically accept the premise that there's something to be afraid of. You have to lead them to it.

We saw how the local newsies do it. They'll cover conditions like terrifying turbulence, conditions that they know aren't really going to be a problem for most people. To keep things honest, they'll tell you as much in their reports, only they'll temper reassuring language with frightening language to keep us on board for the bumpy ride.

The networks are playing at a different level. They have a national audience, a discerning audience that rightly expects to be frightened by conditions they have a reasonable chance of experiencing.

Like car theft.

It's scary to think of what could happen if your car was stolen. You might wonder whether you would get it back, or where it might end up. Thinking about it could generate "a feeling of alarm or disquiet caused by the expectation of danger, or the like; terror; dread; apprehension." That's the desired effect.

A good time to run the story would be following an official announcement about how car theft is on the rise. Then, you could draw the connection between all those abstract cars that are stolen and the possibility that your particular car will be stolen. It's a big assignment, so you might need once again to go "In Depth."

Tom: *NBC News "In Depth": The traffic in stolen cars. What happens after your car is driven away by thieves?*

Tom makes it sound as though it's happening to you right now.

Tom: *Vehicle theft in this country costs Americans more than $7 billion every year. But where do those hot wheels go? We begin tonight's "In Depth" reporting with NBC's Pete Williams.*

Pete shows us action footage of Miami police and FBI agents prowling the streets just before dawn, looking for stolen cars. We're comforted that professionals are at work to help us, and there is something romantic about the fact that it's just before dawn. Still, we're alarmed at the frustration they're expressing at their inability to recover many of the cars that are taken.

This would be a good time for Pete to introduce those statistics, to tell us how bad the problem has become.

Pete: *Car theft remains America's most expensive property crime, one every 23 seconds, adding up to almost one-and-a-half million stolen cars a year. And while that number is down over the past decade, police actually recover far fewer cars now.*

Can we rewind the tape and listen to that again?

Pete: *And while that number is down over the past decade, police actually recover far fewer cars now.*

It goes by quickly, but the on-screen graphic says "Down About 19%."

Pete: *One-third of them are never found.*

That's a scary way of saying two-thirds of them are.

In other words, car thefts are down nineteen percent over the past decade, and two of every three stolen cars are recovered. You could write the story that way, but why would you? The difference is just a variation in the way you interpret statistics, and everyone knows how easily manipulated statistics are.

If this were an outrage story, the statistical interpretation would be very important. Remember, outrage stories are rational. Statistics are rational. Fear stories are primal.

Pete's interpretation of the car theft figures allows him to set up such observations as, *the FBI believes half the missing cars wind up in foreign countries, everywhere from Mexico City to Moscow, Peru to Pakistan.* That's much scarier than saying "two-thirds of all missing cars end up back in your driveway in places like Akron and Kansas City." It's more exotic, too.

It permits him to have an FBI agent say, *We've recovered 'em in forty-nine different countries, there's no rhyme or reason.*

It justifies Pete saying, *In Los Angeles, this undercover police detective says car smugglers try hiding stolen cars underneath cargo headed for Thailand, switching vehicle numbers on stolen Mercedes cars for buyers in Russia, or concealing cars behind false panels in shipments of toilets bound for China.*

Pete wants you to imagine your Mercedes stuffed behind a big shipment of toilets, never to be seen again. He wants you to fear that *U.S. criminal penalties for car thieves who supply the smugglers are not very tough.* He wants you to worry that *when the pros steal your car, you may never see it again.*

If Pete hadn't told you this, you might never have realized it. Which is why they call it "news."

6:18:00 PM: SCARY PHONES

Dan: *Tonight's "Eye on America" investigates a supposed improvement on an old invention, and what could be a dangerous new side-effect.*

This is a classic opening to a fear story. The invention is old, familiar. But improvements—supposed improvements—threaten to disrupt our sense of comfort. There could be side-effects. Who isn't a little afraid of technology, especially when the supposed improvement could be dangerous?

Dan really knows how to cut to the heart of it. That's why he's one of the most trusted people in America.

Dan: *CBS's Sandra Hughes has a preview of new research and new questions about cell phones and cancer.*

A full-screen graphic of a U.S. flag imprinted with the CBS logo proclaims this to be an "Eye on America Investigation." That's another way of saying Sandra's report will be "In Depth."

Fear stories invite a lot of special notice.

Sandra: *Cell phones are no longer a symbol of affluence but a must-have form of communication.*

Well, for television correspondents, at least.

Sandra: *Yet, at a time when the mobile-phone industry is exploding, there is renewed concern over how safe the phones are. Because they're held directly to the head and emit electromagnetic radiation, there has been debate over possible health effects. So, six years ago the cell-phone industry commissioned a $25-million study to prove they are safe.*

That's the official announcement.

Sandra: *Preliminary results of that study are far from conclusive and, if anything, raise more questions.*

And that's our cue to start worrying.

Sandra: *They suggest a possible correlation between cell-phone use and a specific type of brain cancer. The director of the study said the data is not cause for panic, only for more research.*

That's our cue to panic.

Sandra: *The editor of an industry publication says consumers should be outraged.*

Sandra is dangerously close to turning this into an outrage story. But, she pulls back in time.

Louis Slesin, the editor of *Microwave News,* takes 4 seconds to say, *Basically, the industry has not honored its commitment to the American public to get to the bottom of this.*

On the other hand...

Sandra: *The cell-phone industry vigorously defends its research as fair and independent.*

Tom Wheeler is identified as a cell-phone industry spokesman. He says, *The preponderance of evidence as reviewed by the major regulatory bodies in this country, in Canada, in the U.K., international bodies, says that there's not a linkage between the use of wireless phones and health effects.*

Even though Tom gets a monstrous amount of time to tell his side of the story, we can't really believe a spokesman for an industry that has a huge economic interest in whether cell phones cause cancer. The weight of the evidence is becoming clear. We may not have achieved terror or dread, but we're certainly nearing apprehension.

But, what about other research?

Sandra: *Many studies have found no health risks.*

Clearly, Sandra shouldn't go there, because she's done such a good job establishing apprehension. Instead, how about featuring that recent Swedish study?

Sandra: *A recent Swedish study found cell-phone users were two-and-a-half times more likely to suffer brain tumors near their phone ear.*

Anything else?

Sandra: *And Stephen Cleary has found microwaves like those emitted from a cell phone cause cancer cells to grow.*

Maybe the problem we have right now is there isn't enough information to know exactly what the negative aspects of this exposure would be.

Dr. Stephen Cleary: *The problem we have right now is there isn't enough information to know exactly what the negative aspects of this exposure would be.*

But that's okay. If the facts are inconclusive, fear stories can always survive on uncertainty.

Sandra: *The Food and Drug Administration has seen the industry study and will only say it looks like more research is needed, putting consumers right back where they were six years ago, tied to a technology that could be dangerous to their health. In Long Beach, California, this is Sandra Hughes for "Eye on America."*

6:20:00 PM: FEELING FLEECED

We've sampled fear, now let's try outrage. Put down your cell phone and lock your car. It's time to be grossly offended.

One of the most reliable places to turn for outrage is an NBC feature called "The Fleecing of America," which runs regularly on Tom's newscast. It emphasizes ways we're being ripped off, generally through government waste and other boondoggles. The name itself points us to outrage. America is being fleeced. It's offensive.

It's nice to have a reliable place to turn for outrage stories. Actual news events will have an ebb and flow, sometimes generating a lot of outrageous news and sometimes producing very little. But with the availability of a regular feature like "The Fleecing of America," we know we can always look forward to a steady supply of outrage no matter what's happening in the news itself. After all, there's always a government agency somewhere spending too much money on dumb things.

Because of its regular presence in the newscast, there are lots of good fleecing stories, and I wouldn't want to pretend that any one in particular is best. They generally start with a set-up designed to get you going, then come in with a punch line that triggers the outrage.

Here's a quick example from a follow-up report to a four-year-old fleecing story on an *ornate and controversial federal courthouse in*

Boston, which is finally open for business, along with—here's the set-up—*its boat dock, eight-story atrium, and carved engravings.*

We're looking at pictures of a federal building that looks a little like a luxury hotel.

My sense of decency, morality, and good taste has been offended, and I'm ready for more. NBC correspondent Rehema Ellis reminds us that *you may remember it was almost $100 million over budget,* although after four years you would be forgiven if you didn't get the figure exactly right. So, how high was the final price tag?—$227 million. Now, the real punch line: *Some advocates say that despite the obvious attention to detail, something major fell way short: access for the handicapped. A veterans' group claims the federal government doesn't meet federal guidelines for providing total access for the disabled.*

They can remember the carved engravings, but they forgot the ramps. Can the government explain this? Of course, it can't.

Thurman Davis (General Services Administration): *When the building was designed, we felt that we were in compliance, but there have been many changes since that time.*

So, the government will have to pour still more money into the courthouse. The additional cost: $700 thousand.

Even though $700 thousand is mere pocket change from the federal budget, it's lots of money to you and me. We realize we all would have been better off if the feds hadn't been so busy worrying about spending money on docks and had gotten the important stuff right the first time. We have reason to be outraged.

We feel fleeced.

That's how it works.

Now, here's tonight's story about another branch of government thoroughly out of control. We'll let Tom do the set-up.

Tom: *Now, "The Fleecing of America" and a federal agency already under fire for allowing nuclear secrets to be leaked to the Chinese.*

Leaking nuclear secrets to the Chinese sounds pretty bad. But that's nothing compared to wasting taxpayer money.

Tom: *Now, there are new revelations that the Energy Department is also cited for wasting taxpayer money on extensive and out of control travel costs, even after it promised to get those costs under control. Here's NBC's Lisa Myers.*

They're still up to it, even after having been warned, even after promising to get it right. It all makes for a particularly effective set-up.

Lisa: *A high-flying federal agency blasted by government investigators for out of control travel costs.*

The "high-flying" part is underscored with a picture of an airplane taking off. It beautifully illustrates the idea of travel costs taking off—a nice touch.

Then, to heighten our suspense, Lisa plays a guessing game.

Lisa: *Is it the State Department? No. The Pentagon? No. It's the Department of Energy, which four years ago promised to dramatically cut travel costs for workers at its research labs.*

Did it?

Lisa: *It did—for a year. But government investigators now say these travel costs alone reached almost a quarter of a billion dollars last year, $23 million more than promised.*

A graphic of a price tag bearing the figure "$243 million" appears in front of another picture of an airplane taking off. It's a big number, although a quarter of a billion sounds bigger. Now, the disputed amount—the $23-million overrun—isn't nearly that high. But the precise figure is less important than the outrage it generates, and everybody knows $243 million buys a lot more outrage than $23 million.

Besides, it gets worse.

Lisa: *It gets worse. Some workers at government labs weren't even told to save money.*

That's the punch line.

Victor Rezendes (General Accounting Office): *At Los Alamos, we found that the contractor was not even aware that the department was trying to minimize travel costs.*

Lisa: *In fact, the Department of Energy paid to send sixty-four researchers from Los Alamos to Vancouver, British Columbia. And they were only part of a group of 525 researchers who came here for a conference on particle acceleration.*

Did I hear Lisa correctly? Did she say 525 government scientists discussing particle acceleration?

Lisa: *That's right—525 government scientists discussing particle acceleration. That's enough to fill this auditorium more than three times over.* Lisa is standing in the middle of a large auditorium. *And you paid for it. How much? A million dollars.*

Now, I don't know very much about particle acceleration, and I imagine Lisa doesn't, either. But a million dollars sounds like a pretty big price to pay for 525 scientists to talk about it. Maybe some of those researchers could have stayed home. Lisa's thinking the same way.

Lisa: *Wouldn't 200 or 300 scientists have been enough?*

Fulvia Pilat is an accelerator physicist. She probably knows a lot about particle acceleration. And she thinks Lisa's just pulling numbers out of the air.

Fulvia Pilat: *It's very important for the people to be there, because they know that everybody who is relevant or knowledgeable in the field will be there.*

That sounds like a reasonable position, and it was fair of Lisa to present it. Maybe the conference even had a beneficial purpose, sort of like an expensive investment that returns something. But if we dwell on it too much, it will undermine the punch line. So, Lisa shifts the subject slightly, to other spending.

Lisa: *Investigators also criticize other spending. Taxpayers picked up the tab for liquor and entertainment at some conferences, including a concert by cellist Yo Yo Ma. Also paid travel costs, hotels, and rental cars, so contractors could earn master's degrees.*

And what is the Energy Department doing about this?

Lisa: *The Energy Department says it's taking steps to control these costs...*

Haven't we heard that somewhere before?

Lisa: *...and promises to do better, just as it promised four years ago.*

T.J. Glauthier (Deputy Secretary of Energy): *We ask you to follow us, watch this, and we'll see what we can deliver.*

What else can he say?

Lisa (to T.J.): *Some critics say your department has done about as well managing taxpayer dollars as it has protecting the nation's nuclear secrets.*

Ouch.

T.J.: *Well, we're making a lot of changes in both areas.*

Lisa: *Still, some critics call the Energy Department the worst-managed agency in government, and say it's time to ground this "Fleecing of America."*

The plane that was taking off earlier when Lisa was talking about soaring costs is now landing on the runway, with our outrage safely stowed in the overhead compartments.

The government is a favorite subject of fleecing stories, where the point usually is that you can't trust a large and impersonal bureaucracy to do the responsible thing, particularly when it comes to managing money. So, even if there are other departments that are better managed than the Department of Energy, they'll never be featured in the news because a well-managed bureaucracy is boring to watch, not to mention counterintuitive to imagine.

It would be unfair, though, to suggest that the network newsies are picking on the government or taking its problems out of proportion. Nothing could be further from the truth. Large private bureaucracies can also be the subject of critical, outrage-inducing reports. Focusing on corporations trying to get the best of us equalizes the fleecing reports by supplying us with a well-balanced basis for our outrage.

All corporations are in play, provided, of course, that they do not pose an obvious conflict of interest with outrage coverage, such as if the corporation happens to own one of the television networks. But this shouldn't create much of an obstacle for producers, because very few corporations actually own a network. There are many good private bureaucracies to choose from—the airlines, for example.

Nobody likes the airlines, except maybe the travel agents working for the Department of Energy. So, when the airline industry offers a *preemptive strike* to combat *growing complaints about air travel,* we have a great set-up for another outrage story. They want to take matters into their own hands and offer *a voluntary plan to satisfy the public and angry members of Congress.* Tom tells us the airlines *are promising to put customers first.*

Tom must be pretty gullible if he believes it. Robert Hager can offer a more reasonable explanation of what's going on. Better than that, he can offer prefabricated outrage.

Robert: *Seems almost everyone has a horror story about air travel recently.*

Man (at airline ticket counter, yelling at agent): *Your obligation was to get me here at a specific time! You failed to do so!*

Another Man: *You're stuck, you're there, you're at their mercy. So, you're playing by their rules all of a sudden. You have no rules, you have in a sense, we're talking about no rights.*

Still Another Man: *It seems like there's no rhyme or reason for why the prices are one time different and one time not. It doesn't make any sense to me.*

And these people didn't even experience Terrifying Turbulence.

Robert: *Today, the airline industry promises to try to do better.*

Haven't we heard that somewhere before?

Robert: *The airlines promise to offer ticket-buyers the lowest price available; permit passengers to cancel a ticket within 24 hours of purchase without penalty; notify passengers quickly of flight delays or cancellations and explain why; answer any written complaint from passengers within two months; and for long delays on the runway, make sure enough food and water are available.*

We're probably also supposed to believe that the food will taste good. There has to be a catch. Robert explains.

Robert: *The airlines are attempting to preempt congressional threats of a tough new law. But in congress today, some called the new plan hot air, promises that will soon be broken. Senator Ron Wyden:*

Ron: *This is a wink and a nod to try to convince people that they're going to be accountable for better service standards, and the reality is there's not much there, there.*

Robert: *True, say many skeptical passengers.*

Skeptical Passenger: *They just don't care.*

Robert: *But now the airlines promise reform.*

Airline President: *We really do care.*

It's the skeptical passenger we can identify with versus the airline president who's trying to avoid government regulations. Which one do you believe?

Robert: *And the government says it will be watching them, seeing whether the airlines stick to their plan and make life easier for weary travelers.*

This is momentarily comforting, until we realize that the government that's going to be watching them is the same government that can't seem to figure out how to put handicapped access in a courthouse. And that ultimately is the greatest benefit of outrage stories: They leave us frustrated with government and industry.

It's why we're fortunate to have Dan and Peter and Tom. Without them, we wouldn't have anyone to trust.

6:22:30 PM: TEASE

Still ahead on "The CBS Evening News," Weatherwatch: Pelting from the sky—freak hail bops Texas.

6:22:35 PM: PROMO

Tomorrow—has your pension plan been robbed? When is the last time you checked? Is your money safe? Watch ABC's "World News Tonight," with Peter Jennings.

Does he look like a guy who could take a bank for $350 million? It was so easy, you have to wonder why everybody doesn't do it. Sunday, on "Sixty Minutes."

On the next "Extra!"—It's supposed to ease the pain of childbirth, not change your life forever. "Extra!" exposes the potential dangers of the routine epidural, and shows you how you can reduce your risk. Then— what does an ex-con who bombed abortion clinics have in common with Kathie Lee Gifford? A piece of Kathie's past, next "Extra!"

6:23:00 PM: AD TIME-OUT: TAKE THE FEAR AND OUTRAGE CHALLENGE!

Now that you've had a first-hand experience with network-generated fear and outrage, it's time to put your knowledge to the test. See if you've become a sophisticated viewer. See how well you can distinguish disquiet from disgust.

Take the "Fear and Outrage Challenge!"

Here's how it works: In a few seconds, Dan will introduce a story that ran just following this time slot, at 6:26 PM, on another day. It has the potential to invoke fear or outrage, to move our hearts or to reach our minds. Your mission is to figure out which it does, to classify this story the way a pro would.

It won't be easy, because this story is far from clear cut. Let's hear it in its entirety, then we'll go through it together.

The opening graphic contains the ominous statement: "Broken Dreams." Dan waxes poetic.

Dan: *The Bible tells the story of a man who built his house on the sand, and it fell, and "great was the fall of it." The same thing happened today to some homeowners in Philadelphia. CBS's Jeffrey Kofman reports.*

Jeffrey: *On Hagerman Street today, they took down the flag for the last time.*

Male Homeowner: *My American dream is going down with that house.*

Bricks crash to the ground.

Jeffrey: *Brick by brick, city crews began tearing apart a dozen houses.* More bricks crash to the ground. *The city condemned the leaning houses on Hagerman after some were found to be tilting almost a foot.* Many more bricks crash down.

Female Homeowner: *If you put a ball in the dining room, it would literally roll down into your living room.*

Jeffrey: *The city offered little help, leaving residents with a sinking feeling as they discovered insurance wouldn't help them either. When they built Hagerman Street seventy years ago, this was an old creek bed that they filled with twenty-one feet of ash. The city said the ash was eroding away, and the city insisted that is what was causing this.*

Jeffrey points to the sinking homes behind him.

Jeffrey: *People complained that Mayor Ed Rendell found time this week to unveil his own hoagie, the Rendelli, but he didn't have time for the homeowners on Hagerman.*

A sign for the Rendelli features the mayor's smiling face. We notice the sandwich has provolone cheese and sweet peppers. The camera pans right, and there's the mayor wearing an apron, making a Rendelli.

But then one resident dug up his three-year-old home video showing it may have been the city's fault. It showed a flooded roadbed and houses being shored up during sewer construction.

A home video confirms Jeffrey's observations.

Mayor Rendell (without apron): *We hope to have checks in the hands of the residents within a ten-day period.*

Jeffrey: *Perhaps embarrassed by the hoagie and certainly feeling the heat, this afternoon the mayor relented and took responsibility.*

Jeffrey (to male resident): *When people say you can't fight city hall, what do you say?*

Male Resident: *I guess you can if you have a videotape.*

Jeffrey: *Tonight, Hagerman's a street of broken houses, but no longer a street of broken dreams. Jeffrey Kofman, CBS News, Philadelphia.*

So, which is it—fear or outrage? Before you answer, let's go through the story again together.

The story starts with the potential to be either—or both.

My American dream is going down with that house.

Brick by brick, city crews began tearing apart a dozen houses.

We're outraged that the city is tearing down these houses, tearing down dreams. At first, we don't know why they're doing it, but because the government is involved, there could be any reason. It could be a Department of Energy directive.

Then we learn: *The city condemned the leaning houses on Hagerman after some were found to be tilting almost a foot.*

We wonder why the houses are tilting. If we're skilled viewers, we begin to wonder if such a thing could happen to our houses. It triggers a little fear.

However, fear quickly turns back to outrage, both at government—*because the city offered little help*—and at private insurance companies, because they *wouldn't help either*. It's dual outrage, directed at our two favorite targets, the public sector and the private sector.

But wait—we're back to fear when we find out the reason the houses are tilted: *When they built Hagerman Street seventy years ago, this was an old creek bed that they filled with twenty-one feet of ash. The city said the ash was eroding away, and the city insisted that is what was causing this.* Any longtime news viewer would have to wonder, is my house built on ash? Will the ground under it erode one day?

At this point, the choice between fear and outrage is still a complex one. But the story rapidly sorts itself out.

People complained that Mayor Ed Rendell found time this week to unveil his own hoagie, the Rendelli, but he didn't have time for the homeowners on Hagerman.

That's just maddening. How can the mayor sit idly by, wielding hot peppers, while the houses of Hagerman Street tumble under the weight of city wrecking balls? If one of the residents hadn't been smart enough to videotape that sewer construction, would the mayor have been content to spend the week posing for pictures with his hoagie?

It would seem as if this story is headed straight for outrage. Then it happened...

Perhaps embarrassed by the hoagie and certainly feeling the heat, this afternoon the mayor relented and took responsibility.

Jeffrey (to male resident): *When people say you can't fight city hall, what do you say?*

Male Resident: *I guess you can if you have a videotape.*

Things worked out. The mayor responded. The residents won. No outrage. No fear.

This isn't a fear or outrage story after all. The time in the broadcast— 6:26 PM—should have given it away. Everyone is going to live happily ever after. This is dessert.

Tonight, Hagerman's a street of broken houses, but no longer a street of broken dreams.

In a manner most appropriate for television, videotape had saved the day. It brought the powerful forces of government around to the side of the little guy, dampening outrage and alleviating fears.

There is no more fitting way to end a television newscast.

6:26:00 PM: FREAKY, ROOF-BUSTING GREAT BALLS OF HAIL

Except possibly with more weather. There can never be too much weather.

On the CBS Weatherwatch, they sure could use some improved storm warnings in the Texas panhandle. Freak hailstorms have battered farms, farmers, and their cars back to the Ice Age.

In the end, there is weather because, as in the beginning, there are pictures.

Pictures of hailstones beating against a car window:

In the Texas panhandle, they're getting bombarded.

Pictures of hail accumulating on the highway:

Hail. Twice in three weeks. Road-smothering, roof-busting, wall-chipping hail.

Pictures of hail bouncing off walls and rooftops:

Texas-size chunks of ice, pummeling everyone and everything in its path at speeds up to a hundred miles an hour.

Without pictures, darkness would cover the face of the screen.

Pictures of hailstones the size of baseballs:

Farmers are scrambling to replant. New crops right on top of the shredded wheat they had no time to clear.

Pictures of fields flattened by hail:

There is no rhyme or reason any forecasters see, other than it's spring, it's Texas, and man's not in charge.

Pictures of car windows shattered by hail:

Lair's car lot looks like a rifle range. Cars and trucks, beaten and battered, nailed and hammered.

With pictures, there is light. Dan saw the pictures.

A huge storm cloud gathers on the horizon.

And Dan saw that the pictures were good.

6:28:30 PM: PROMO

Dan: *And that's part of our world tonight. I'll be back later here on CBS with "48 Hours." Erin Moriarty has a preview for you.*

Erin: *Should a child have the right to choose her family?*

Samantha: *I've been in, like, four homes already.*

Erin: *Only one can have her.*

Mom: *I just want to be her mommy.*

Erin: *But two families want her.*

Other Mom: *She's trying to rob my daughter from me.*

Erin: *Samantha's choice, later on "48 Hours."*

6:28:50 PM: PROMO

Dan: *Until "48 Hours" at ten o'clock, nine Central Time, Dan Rather reporting for "The CBS Evening News." See you later.*

Disembodied Voice: *Experience you can trust—CBS News.*

6:29:00 PM: PROMO

An all new "Dateline."

O.J.: *Why don't you ask me?*

Voice: *I just did. Where were you?*

O.J.: *Why don't you ask me?*

You may think you've seen all there is on O.J. Simpson, but "Dateline's" got something you haven't seen.

O.J.: *Never once did I ever hit her with my fist. Ever.*

The O.J. Simpson deposition. A "Dateline" exclusive. Tuesday at ten, nine Central on NBC.

6:29:15 PM: PROMO

Sunday—How safe are America's nuclear secrets? Plus Matalin and Carville square off on Decision 2000, on "Meet the Press."

6:29:20 PM: PROMO

This has been a presentation of NBC News. More Americans watch NBC News than any other news organization in the world.

6:29:25 PM: PROMO

On the next "Extra!" It's one of Tinseltown's biggest mysteries. A beautiful cheerleader with dreams of stardom comes to L.A. to be crowned Miss Hollywood. Then, she's found brutally murdered. No clues. No leads. "Extra!" reopens the case and asks you—who killed Miss Hollywood?

6:29:40 PM: PROMO

A TV mascot fights for his life when savagely attacked by a crazed kangaroo. Tonight on "The World's Most Amazing Videos."

6:29:45 PM: PROMO

This has been a presentation of ABC News. More Americans get their news from ABC News than from any other source.

6:29:50 PM: PROMO

Crime writer Aphrodite Jones takes you into a bizarre world of teenage vampires, where obsessions with blood rituals end in murder. The dark world of teenage vampires, on the next "Montel."

6:29:59 PM: FADE OUT

Postscript: The Sky Keeps Falling

9:59:15 PM: NEWS

Meteorites. Scientists say they wiped out the dinosaurs. Now could they change the face of the earth again? It's no TV movie. "Dateline" next on NBC.

9:59:30 PM: TV SHOW

On our next "Unsolved Mysteries." In 1994, fragments of a giant comet set off a series of cataclysmic explosions on the planet Jupiter. Is there more destruction lurking in the night sky? Will Earth be the next target? Join me next time for another intriguing edition of "Unsolved Mysteries."

9:59:45 PM: MINI-SERIES

Brace yourself for February's biggest event. Scientists say that there are millions of asteroids on a collision course with Earth. Among them there's an asteroid big enough, powerful enough to end all life on the planet. If we knew it was coming could we stop it? The truth will surprise you. One week from Sunday, the sky is falling when "Asteroid" hits on NBC.

The stories you want to hear. The news you need to know. "Dateline NBC" is next.

10:00:00 PM: NEWS

This is "Dateline." Tonight: They can show up as silver streaks in the night or smash into the earth with explosive force. How much do we know about what's out there? A "Dateline"/Discovery Channel exclusive.

10:27:30 PM: NEWS

Coming up: They may be a science-fiction hit, but when it comes to large asteroids, one strike could mean you're out. Lumps of rock the size of skyscrapers would start raining down upon Washington. It may be a long shot, but should we be concerned?

10:34:00 PM: NEWS

We've been hearing a lot about asteroids lately, about what could happen if a giant asteroid hit the earth. In fact, we may be the third rock from the sun, but there are plenty of others hurtling around. Tonight, in a "Dateline"/Discovery Channel exclusive, we ask, should we be worried?

Here is our worst nightmare. Scientists say this could happen. An asteroid six miles wide streaks toward earth at seventy times the speed of sound. The nightmare rock hits New York City. Eight-million souls are wiped off the face of the earth. The impact creates a crater one hundred miles wide. Shock waves pulse outward. Lumps of rock the size of skyscrapers would start raining down upon Washington 30 or 40 seconds later. Chicago would get similar size rocks two or three minutes after that. Los Angeles and San Francisco, another 5 minutes later. It truly would be calamitous for the whole of North America, indeed the whole of the world. What isn't leveled by the blast burns in a colossal firestorm. Rocks from the explosion rain down as secondary meteors worldwide. Cities and towns are swallowed up in the flames. Within an hour of impact, ninety-five percent of life on earth perishes. Now, a cosmic winter takes hold and lasts for months. What little plant life is left, what little food, dies. The few people who managed to survive inherit a devastated world, a ruined planet.

But that nightmare wasn't real, that was just animation. And scientists admit the possibility of such a thing occurring in our lifetime or even for thousands of years is very remote.

10:45:20 PM: MINI-SERIES

It has been blamed for the extinction of the dinosaurs. Scientists are wondering—could it happen again?

"We've got thousands of pieces coming at us!"

"My God!"

"There's an asteroid coming right at us!"

"Stay in the basement!"

A week from Sunday—"The inevitable is here!"

The sky is falling. "Asteroid." One week from Sunday.

10:57:15 PM: NEWS

"Dateline NBC." Winner of the Edward R. Murrow award for outstanding investigative reporting. Awarded again and again for excellence in journalism. "Dateline NBC" will be right back.

Closing Comments

The selection of the programs featured was fairly straightforward. One of the assumptions I made was that any program on any network at any time is representative of every program on every network at every time. In that regard, I could have easily selected programs from another week or another month and found examples of the same types of coverage contained in this book. Had I done that, I would have written a book filled with completely different examples, but the general tone and feel of the book would have been unaffected. The words would have been different, but the message would have been the same. Everything would have changed, and nothing would have changed.

This is exactly how television news works. In this regard, the book follows the same formula as the one used by television producers. Every day the particulars of television news—the news stories—are different, but the tone and feel of the newscast remains the same. Even though news events are a variable entity, television news requires consistency to build and hold your loyalty. If you know what to expect from a newscast, you'll become comfortable with it. Producers hope you'll even become a bit dependent on it. They try to achieve that objective by delivering the same type of news stories in the same format with the same personalities every day.

So, the examples I used owe their selection largely to the timing of the book's development. Early in the process, I made video recordings of the same week of local news programs in the four markets featured in the book. It was the week of February 24, 1997, and, with one exception, all the material in the "Live at Five" section of the book comes from local news programs that aired at that time. (The one exception is the 5:37 PM feature on "Extreme Sex," which aired two weeks earlier, but which was too good to pass up.)

Once you get past the specifics, local news stories tend to be about the same assortment of things, and they're things that could happen at any time. So, while it may be interesting to a real news viewer to know which fire, murder, assault, shootout, or accident occurred on any given day, those details are irrelevant to this book. All that matters is that local news presents us with an endless assortment of fire, murder, assault, shootout, and accident stories, along with a host of features about things that are independent of specific events and are therefore not time bound. The local news stories described in this book would be as suitable for air this week as they were three years ago, and as they would have been five or even ten years ago. The local news formula simply has not changed that much.

Although national news also employs a formula, the particulars matter more because our recognition of national figures changes over time. How many of us can remember anything about the Bush administration besides the Persian Gulf War and possibly the recession of 1992? Who really wants to read another word about the O.J. Simpson case? Does anybody remember the Menendez brothers? For this reason, I selected national news stories late in the production cycle of this book to make them as recent, and therefore as familiar, as possible. Except for major past events, like the last presidential election and President Clinton's impeachment, all the network news stories aired during the week of June 14, 1999.

Similarly, talk show subjects are largely interchangeable. The examples featured in this book aired during the week of May 10, 1999. The talk shows themselves were chosen for their prominence in the ratings at the time the book was written.

The selection of the four local markets was based largely on geography. I wanted to represent large markets in all four continental time zones, encompassing the Northeast/Mid-Atlantic region (Philadelphia), the Midwest (Detroit), the South/Southwest (Phoenix), and the West (Los Angeles). I feature one station from each city: the CBS affiliate in Philadelphia (KYW) and ABC affiliates in Detroit (WXYZ), Phoenix (KNXV), and Los Angeles (KABC). Additional stories come from the CBS affiliate in Phoenix and the NBC affiliate in Philadelphia. My thanks to Mary Adler (Detroit), Justin Green and Bob Witkowsic (Phoenix), and Bernice and Darwin Miller (Los Angeles) for their assistance.

I have attempted to represent the stories exactly as they appeared on television. However, I did make minor alterations to a few stories to make them conform to the text (either by changing the tense of a story or clarifying ambiguous references to "it" or "that"). And, some of the tease and segue sections combine dialogue from different newscasts, at times from newscasts in different cities. These changes were made purely for cosmetic purposes, to maintain continuity in the text. None of the changes affect the meaning or intent of the stories, and all the dialogue is real.

The local news stories portrayed in this book originally aired at 11 PM. The decision to modify the air time was made to accommodate the design of this book, which emphasizes the sweep of early evening news. In general, early evening news is similar to late evening news, and some of the stories addressed here aired in the early evening as well. However, some of the more explicit features were intended for late-night viewing, and readers should be advised that local television stations generally act responsibly and reserve some of their more explicit subject matter for late-night hours. The decision to portray some of these late-night stories in an earlier time slot should not be construed as a misrepresentation of this approach; it is simply an editorial decision made for stylistic purposes. Of course, young children with early bedtimes wishing to hear explicit dialogue about adult subjects can always turn to an afternoon talk show.

The stories presented here are offered as prototypical news stories, but there are, of course, exceptions. Some local news reports have attempted to buck the "Live at Five" trend and bolster substance at the expense of splash, sometimes at the cost of decreased viewership and revenues. Similarly, some stations rely more heavily than others on sensational coverage. I have attempted to portray a typical or average newscast, and in that sense what you read should have a familiar feel. But, as with any average, it will not be an exact replica of what you see and hear on your favorite station.

A similar statement may be made about talk shows. "The Jerry Springer Show" may be the most extreme version of the genre and the easiest to parody. But, as of this writing, it is also the most successful syndicated show of its type and, therefore, the most obvious target and best example. Intentionally missing from this book is reference to "The Oprah Winfrey Show," which unlike its tabloid cousins has steadfastly avoided the sort of programming described here. Its absence from the book could make it too easy to forget that responsible programming exists, and that it can command an audience. Like the local news operations that eschew sleaze and embrace a more balanced perspective, Oprah should be remembered—and applauded.

Finally, I would like to offer a brief note of thanks to a few people whose input has been critical in developing this project and turning it into a book: Susan Tolchin, Jeffrey Seller, Andrew Lippa, Jennifer Knerr, Brenda Hadenfeldt, and Susan, Doris, and Sheldon Kerbel. A special debt is owed to my editor Leo Wiegman, who was instrumental in conceptualizing this book's format and without whom this book would still be just a manuscript-in-waiting, and to the outstanding staff at Westview Press for their attentiveness and professionalism. With love and gratitude, I dedicate this book to my wife, Adrienne— who has been with me through four books and whose unwavering support and editorial guidance have made each one possible—and to my daughter, Gabrielle.

About the Author

My media experience is probably typical, if there is such a thing as a typical media experience. And I am familiar with both small and large media markets.

I reported radio news at WINR-AM Binghamton, a small market, during what was called the "morning drive" in a community with too few cars to form a rush hour. The station's slogan—"you never know what will happen next"—vastly exaggerated a programming format that religiously played the same three songs 24 hours a day, but described life at the studio in ways the general manager probably wouldn't like to admit. When the FCC decided radio stations can't leave their transmitters unattended, this station closed its in-town studio and moved everyone to the transmitter shack on an isolated, wind-swept, hilltop location beyond the psychiatric center. I found the studio by driving my car up the dirt road and until the hair on my neck stood up.

Although WINR had a devoted listenership, it was hardly the most popular station in town. That would have been WMRV, a top-forty, FM favorite whose notoriety was probably due to its willingness to play thirty-seven more charted hits than WINR. The entire station was little more than a wall-size tape machine located in a closet, where four reel-to-reel tapes would randomly alternate playing 3-minute cuts identified by an ever-happy, disembodied voice playing on a cartridge. "That was—Barry *Manilow!*" the voice would rave. "Now, here's...Barry *Manilow!*" Once the sign-off cartridge was accidentally activated in the middle of the afternoon, and the station proceeded to sign itself off and on for an hour before a technician noticed. It won the ratings battle in its time slot.

Never knowing what would happen next prepared me to work in New York, a large market, writing the news for a public television news program with an audience so tiny that it showed up in the ratings as an asterisk: too small to measure. The show followed Dick Cavett, who was no longer the Dick Cavett of late-night, prime-time fame, but Cavett on the downhill, making wry jokes with cultural anthropologists as living rooms darkened across Brooklyn. Airing as we did at 11:30 PM, even if Cavett had been popular, we couldn't have competed with reruns of *Maude*.

I became a newswriter after working first as a production associate, a position which I'm certain if ever challenged in court would be struck down as a violation of the constitutional protection against involuntary servitude. The job covered everything from writing copy to getting coffee for the talent, and it came without a paycheck. But it was New York, where plenty of people were waiting in line to find an unpaid television job like mine.

Unpaid was a big thing in public television, as it is everywhere in the industry. "Don't you realize how many people would do your job for nothing?" I remember being told by a PBS human resource manager, who apparently wasn't paying attention.

When I finally landed a well-paying job with CNN, I had seen enough of television from the inside to realize that I was better suited to watching it from afar. And that is what I have been doing, more or less, over the past decade. During that time, I have written about the media and politics while teaching political science at Villanova University, near Philadelphia. The impetus for this book comes from both the newsroom and the classroom, from having been a part of small and large market media and from having seen my students' eyes open a little when we consider different ways to look at the news.

Notes

HOUR ONE: SYNDICATED TALK

4:00:00 PM: STATION IDENTIFICATION
These are real stations and real promotions. Most of the local news reports included in this book appeared on one of these stations during the last couple of years.

4:00:05 PM: OPENING MONTAGE (ROLL TAPE)
The three syndicated programs opened in this way on Thursday, May 13, 1999.

4:00:35 PM: MEET THE HOSTS
The quotations in this section came from the following Web sites:

The Ricki Lake homepage:
> www.spe.sony.com/tv/shows/ricki;

"The Jenny Jones Show" description:
> www.jennyjones.com/cmp/descr.htm;

"About Jenny" biography:
> www.jennyjones.com/cmp/bios.htm;

"The Montel Williams Show" homepage:
> www.paramount.com/tvmontel;

The Jerry Springer homepage:
> www.universalstudios.com/tv/jerryspringer/meetjerry.html;

All About Sally:
> www.sallyjessy.com/bio.html;

All About Sally's Show:

    www.sallyjessy.com/theshow.html;

Dan Rather Biography:

    www.cbs.com/prd1/now/template.display;

Tom Brokaw Biography:

    www.msnbc.com/onair/bios/t_brokaw.asp;

Peter Jennings Biography:

    http://more.abcnews.go.com/onair/worldnewstonight/jennings_
    peter_bio.html.

4:05:00 PM: MEET THE GUESTS

Heaven and company all appeared on Friday, May 14, 1999. The cheaters were on "The Jerry Springer Show," the people with crushes were on "Sally Jessy Raphael," and the paternity questions were settled on "The Montel Williams Show." All information in this section comes from the TV Talk Show Web site, www.tvtalkshows.com.

Monday's cheaters (May 10, 1999) appeared on "Jerry Springer," all threesomes appeared on "The Ricki Lake Show," the jailed ex and the chesty women were on "Sally," and the questionable body parts appeared (to some extent) on "The Jenny Jones Show."

Tuesday's cheaters (May 11, 1999) also appeared on "Jerry Springer." The lie-detector test was on "Jenny Jones," and the lethal spouse was on "Montel Williams."

Wednesday's cheaters (May 12, 1999) also appeared on "Jerry Springer." The wild teens were on "Ricki Lake."

Thursday's cheaters (May 13, 1999) were presented courtesy of Jerry Springer and Ricki Lake. Jenny Jones contributed the makeover and the large-breasted women. The stolen boyfriend appeared on "The Montel Williams Show."

4:10:00 PM: SUPPLY MEDICAL TREATMENT FOR THE GUESTS

Solo, Kimberly, and company appeared on "The Jerry Springer Show" on Monday, May 17, 1999.

HOUR TWO: "LIVE AT FIVE"

5:00:30 PM: INVENTING A RIOT

All stories in this section originally aired in 1997. This story appeared February 26 on KNXV-TV Phoenix.

5:03:00 PM: ONLY POPULAR RESTAURANTS ARE DANGEROUS

This story appeared February 26 on KYW-TV Philadelphia.

5:05:50 PM: TEASE

The tease is a composite that appeared during the week of February 24 on KABC-TV Los Angeles (breast implant story and the weather) and on WXYZ-TV Detroit ("It can happen at any time"). Lisa McRee and Dallas Raines appeared in Los Angeles.

5:06:00 PM: AD TIME-OUT: YOU WILL BE ON TELEVISION

The story appeared on WXYZ-TV Detroit, February 26.

5:12:00 PM: MOVIE—OR REALITY?

This story also appeared on WXYZ-TV Detroit, February 28.

5:15:00 PM: THE GREAT BAKING POWDER INCIDENT

In reality, this story led the news on WXYZ-TV Detroit on February 24. The follow-up aired the next day, 14 minutes into the newscast.

5:15:52 PM: TEASE

This tease ran in Los Angeles, except for the turbulence part, which ran in Detroit.

5:16:00 PM: PROMO

The promo for "Hard Copy" ran on stations where this syndicated program appears. The promo presented here ran along with the stories related in this manuscript during the week of February 24.

5:20:00 PM: FIRST FEATURE: IT COULD HAPPEN ANY TIME WITHOUT WARNING

Viewers in Detroit were treated to this feature on February 26 on WXYZ-TV.

5:23:30 PM: SEGUE INTO TERRIFYING WEATHER

The dialogue is combined from two exchanges between Diana Lewis and Jerry Hodak following the story on "Terrifying Turbulence."

5:29:00 PM: DESSERT

The baby elephant story was broadcast on KYW-TV Philadelphia on February 28; the visually impaired kids and injured wrestler closed the KYW broadcast on February 25. The sea-otter story closed the newscast on KABC-TV Los Angeles, February 26. The restaurant celebration also appeared on February 26 on KYW. It was the same broadcast during which the restaurant murder story appeared.

5:30:00 PM: HOW MANY TIMES CAN ONE CAR SMASH INTO A HOUSE?

This story came from KABC-TV Los Angeles, February 27.

5:31:40 PM: MINOR INJURIES, MAJOR PICTURES

Both stories appeared on Phoenix Channel Five, February 24.

5:32:10 PM: WICKED WINDS

We're back to KABC-TV Los Angeles.

**5:34:00 PM: AD TIME-OUT: MAY IS THE CRUELEST MONTH.
FEBRUARY'S NOT SO GREAT, EITHER**

Nielsen surveys all major markets four times a year—in November, February, May, and July—with the first three sweeps months coinciding with periods of original network programming. For more on the ratings sweeps, see the Nielsen Media Research Web site at www.nielsenmedia.com/sweeps.html.

5:37:00 PM: SECOND FEATURE: EXTREME SEX

This story ran on WCAU-TV Philadelphia on February 13.

5:42:00 PM: AD TIME-OUT: YOU CAN BE A NEWS DIRECTOR

Television ratings are gathered by Nielsen Media Research. Television programs are assigned ratings points, which are used to estimate the size of the audience for a program. A program's share is the percentage of television sets in use that are tuned to a program. For more information on how ratings are calculated, see the Nielsen Media Research Web site, www.nielsenmedia.com/index.html. Q Scores measure audience reaction to celebrities, including television news anchors, and are used by stations to determine the familiarity, credibility, and overall appeal of their talent. For more, see the marketing evaluations Web site at www.qscores.com/index.html.

5:45:00 PM: SCORE!
The sports story about the Red Wings and the Coyotes was reported by Vic Lombardi of the Phoenix CBS affiliate on February 24. The dialogue about the Clippers aired on KABC-TV Los Angeles on February 26. All references in this section to the political preferences of real anchors and feelings of hostility between real politicians are purely fictional.

5:48:30 PM: THIRD FEATURE: IMPLANTS
This story was from KABC-TV Los Angeles, February 26.

5:55:30 PM: MORE SEX, PLEASE
This story came from WXYZ-TV Detroit, February 25.

5:56:00 PM: DAVE LOVES CHEESESTEAKS
Larry and Dave chatted on CBS affiliate KYW-TV Philadelphia on February 24.

5:59:00 PM: LOCK THOSE DOORS—AND COME BACK AT ELEVEN
These are composites of teases and story segments that aired in three cities. From Philadelphia: the weight-loss product (February 26), the missing SEPTA driver, and sex charges against the deacon (February 27); from Detroit: furnace repair (February 25) and the Hollywood shoot-out (February 28); from Phoenix: produce (CBS, February 24) and tongue reattachment (ABC, February 27).

HOUR THREE: NETWORK

6:00:00 PM: TEASE
Unless otherwise indicated, all material in this section aired in 1999. The promo for the soap opera "Passions" and Tom Brokaw's tease

about the Pope's health and stolen cars aired on NBC, Tuesday, June 15. The "World News Tonight" opening is from the June 14 program. Dan Rather's tease of the gun-control and cell-phone stories opened "The CBS Evening News with Dan Rather" on June 17.

6:00:25 PM: WAR STORIES

The gun-control story was the lead item on "The CBS Evening News with Dan Rather" on June 17.

6:02:10 PM: EXCUSE ME?

John Donvan covered the Dole campaign for ABC News. His report on Jack Kemp's refusal to attack the Clinton administration during the vice-presidential debate aired on October 10, 1996. His piece on Dole's reluctance to attack Clinton ran three days later, as did Jeff Greenfield's piece on civility in politics. All stories appeared on ABC.

6:05:00 PM: BUT ENOUGH ABOUT YOU

The story on media interest in the George W. Bush campaign appeared on ABC "World News Tonight" on June 14.

6:07:30 PM: UP NEXT

The two stories in this tease appeared separately on CBS. The tease for the weather story aired on June 18; the tease for the homeowner's nightmare aired on June 17.

6:07:30 PM: PROMO

The "Dateline" and "Extra!" promos ran on June 14. The CNBC promo aired June 18. All three appeared during the "NBC Nightly News with Tom Brokaw."

6:07:45 PM: AD TIME-OUT: LET'S HAVE AN IMPEACHMENT!

The figures on television saturation coverage of the Lewinsky affair are courtesy of Robert Lichter of the Center for Media and Public Affairs in Washington, D.C. The House impeachment managers were referred to as a "Conservative Dream Team" on an NBC News report filed by correspondent Dan Abrams, who also filed the report on

"Team Monica." The Lewinsky makeover story was filed by Alan Boyle for MSNBC on November 17, 1998. A February 12, 1999, MSNBC story pondered whether Clinton had been sufficiently contrite following his acquittal. The reference to "Politically Incorrect" is from a story reported by Tom Curry for MSNBC on February 12, 1999, which also included, "By choosing to appear in these vaudevillian venues, elected officials become mere celebrities." A complete archive of NBC and MSNBC coverage of the Clinton impeachment is available at http://msnbc.com/news/.

6:10:00 PM: AL GORE GETS A SURPRISE MAKEOVER

This story ran June 17 on NBC.

6:12:00 PM: DOWN TO SIZE

This story ran immediately after the Gore makeover.

6:13:35 PM: TEASE

The "Fleecing of America" is a regular segment on "NBC Nightly News," and promos for it such as the one featured here are commonplace. This particular one ran June 14.

6:13:40 PM: PROMO

The "Entertainment Tonight" promo was modified from the introduction to the June 17 program. The KYW promo aired the same day in Philadelphia.

6:16:00 PM: SCARY CARS

NBC aired this report on June 15.

6:18:00 PM: SCARY PHONES

This story was broadcast by CBS on June 17.

6:20:00 PM: FEELING FLEECED

All three stories were broadcast on NBC. The courthouse story ran as part of a "Fleecing of America" segment on June 14; the other two stories aired June 18.

6:22:30 PM: TEASE

CBS teased the "hail bops" on June 18.

6:22:35 PM: PROMO

The pension plan promo ran June 14 on ABC, while the "Sixty Minutes" promo aired June 18 on CBS. The promo for "Extra!" is from the June 16 Philadelphia broadcast of ABC "World News Tonight."

6:23:00 PM: AD TIME-OUT: TAKE THE FEAR AND OUTRAGE CHALLENGE!

Sinking homes closed the June 17 edition of "The CBS Evening News."

6:26:00 PM: FREAKY, ROOF-BUSTING GREAT BALLS OF HAIL

The hail story was reported on June 18 by Jim Axelrod on "The CBS Evening News."

6:28:30 PM.– 6:29:50 PM: PROMOS

The promos included here ran on NBC as follows: "Dateline" promo, June 15; "Meet the Press" promo, June 19; "Extra!" promo, June 14; "The World's Most Amazing Videos" promo, July 14; and "Montel" promo, June 19.

POSTSCRIPT: THE SKY KEEPS FALLING

This edition of "Dateline NBC" aired February 7, 1997, during the ratings sweep. The promos for the NBC mini-series ran exactly as depicted, as did the promo for the asteroid segment on the upcoming edition of "Unsolved Mysteries." The promo for "Dateline NBC" that closed the Postscript ran midway through the "Dateline NBC" broadcast.

Index